Angels, Beggars and Castaway Things

Angels, Beggars and Castaway Things

A Forager's Journey Home

Jerry Freeman

Mushika Publications
Post Office Box One
North Windham, Connecticut 06256

Cover design: George Foster, www.fostercovers.com
Copy editing: Jo Hemmant
Mushika logo art: Karen Kiser

Author correspondence: jerry@freemanwhistles.com
Jerry Freeman tweaked whistles are available through
www.freemanwhistles.com

ISBN-13: 978-0692090626

Library of Congress Control Number: 2018903304

for Ana, Arleen and Jim
and the Amish families of northern New York

with heartfelt gratitude
to the New Haven Animal Shelter

dog (dôg), noun: A voice-activated, self-propelled apparatus for determining the exact center of any bed.

Like most of my life, this book is an assemblage of found objects, foraged material pulled from roadsides and dumpsters on the spur of a moment, then reshaped for utility or amusement. Usually both.

There will be another book. Unlike this one, it will be purposefully planned, carefully crafted. But that book I will have to finish actually writing. This book, I did not write. I found it among the random musings that, day by day, have come unbidden and of their own volition coalesced into words.

Or perhaps I should say others found it, pointed it out to me and asked, "Are you writing a book?"

Well, no.

But now that this book has in fact written itself, I invite you to join me here among its pages. I've read it myself and was surprised to find there's an entire, magical world inside. Come in. You'll like it there, I promise.

Some believe
it is only great power
that can hold evil in check,
but that is not what I have found.
It is the small everyday deeds of ordinary folk
that keep the darkness at bay.
Small acts of kindness
and love.

~ *J.R.R. Tolkien*

Prologue

After nine years in rural northern New York, Arleen wanted to come home. We knew it would cost too much to live in the part of Connecticut where she grew up. You can commute to Manhattan from there, which over the years has skyrocketed the real estate prices. So we looked in the part of the state farthest from the City and found a big house on three acres of recently converted farmland.

Built in 2005, the house and land hadn't much character when we moved there in 2008, but I felt they did have promise.

I had insisted we find a house with a walkout basement so I could set up my metalworking shop. The walkout basement would allow me to bring machinery and materials directly in without having to take them through the house and down a flight of stairs.

I made several trips between the old and new homesteads, pulling the five-by-nine utility trailer I'd made by welding together the remains of a snowmobile trailer and a 1960's popup camper. I hauled it behind my 1998 manual transmission Honda Accord, which by then had over 160,000 miles.

After one of the trips, the engine started overheating badly. Blown head gasket. I would have to replace the car. I asked the mechanic, "By chance, do you know anyone who wants to sell a Volkswagen diesel Jetta?" That was my dream car,* much more suited to my needs than the Accord, which had performed heroically nonetheless.

"Come to think of it, I do," he said. He wrote down a name and phone number. "I can't vouch for the car. You'll have to check it out yourself."

I called the seller, an engineer at Pratt and Whitney. It was a 2000 Jetta GLS TDI diesel Volkswagen. "Manual transmission?" I asked. The automatic transmission on those cars was prone to failure, and I wanted to pull loads with it. "Yes, manual transmission." "Why are you selling it?" "I don't want to sell it, but I'm getting transferred to Singapore." He agreed to a price of thirty five hundred dollars.

That's kind of how things work for me. Disaster ALWAYS leads to renewal. It never fails (knock on wood).

To the Connecticut house's walkout basement I moved my machinist lathe, mill/drill machine, metal-cutting band saw and other equipment, along with the materials I'd accumulated for my craft. I installed a dedicated wiring circuit, and high on a wall, a key-operated switch that turns off the whole shop so no machine can be accidentally switched on by a curious child.

I partitioned the two-car garage, creating a small woodworking shop in my half and leaving the other half for the rest of the household. I brought in a 30-amp, 240-volt single-phase circuit so I could run my three-horsepower, 10-inch Grizzly table saw, my eight-inch Reliant jointer and my 12-inch 1950's Parks thickness planer. That planer is a powerhouse workhorse I paid $225 for at a flea market years ago. It's why I love old machines.

I sold my 10-inch Sears radial saw back in New York, then picked up another one here for $100. By the road near our house, someone left some torn-out countertops from which I made the 11-foot radial saw bench where I do most of my crosscutting.

Note: Although moving and setting up my wood shop took only two paragraphs to tell, it took years to accomplish. The metalworking shop, I set up right away because I couldn't make a living without it.

There were several months when I spent most of my time at the old place, getting it in shape to sell and liquidating my business there. In addition to

---

* This was before VW began to falsify emissions information. Of all the years VW has made diesel cars, the manual transmission, 1999 – 2003 model stands out as an exceptionally good car. I wouldn't want any other year.

making musical instruments, which I could move to Connecticut, I bought, renovated and sold house trailers, which I couldn't move and had to shut down.

In the cold months while I was there alone, I burned wood in the fireplace insert to make some heat downstairs. Our Amish neighbor, Reuben Hershberger, was kind to sell me the barkwood scraps from his sawmill for cheap. I couldn't afford heating oil, so I set the thermostat as low as I dared without freezing the pipes. I'm sensitive to smoke and couldn't sleep near the fire, so it was forty-four degrees in the room where I slept.

While I was away, Arleen and the girls carried on as best they could. Arleen was working full time and she was exhausted. One day she told me, a landscaper driving by had seen the tall grass and knocked on the door. "Three acres. To mow it, you've got a $250 lawn there, lady." He suggested a maintenance contract for him to mow every ten days to two weeks. Arleen politely declined.

I don't remember when we met our neighbor Jim but it was our $250 lawn that brought him to our door, just as it had brought the landscaper. As it happens, Jim has cows. Before there was a house on this lot, it was a hay field. Jim talked about how he'd enjoyed the view over the hay field for twenty years before a contractor bought the property and began to dig it up. It made him sad to see, he said.

"Would you mind if I mow the lot and take the hay?" That was the day this land began to come alive again.

Arleen made it clear from the beginning, there would be a houseful of adopted children. That wasn't something I'd ever considered, but I understood it was non-negotiable. Eventually, there were nine, all girls. Right in the middle was Anastasia.

The word that comes to mind is "waif."

Ana was abandoned at birth and languished in an understaffed hospital in Siberia for six months before going to the orphanage, where there wasn't enough food. At age three, when Arleen found Ana's listing during one of her late-night Internet searches, Ana weighed eighteen pounds.

By then, Arleen had showed me pictures of dozens of children up for adoption in various parts of the world. Sometimes I would have a strong feeling about one or another of them, but Ana was altogether different. Her picture pulled at my heart with a power I could not deny. In her eye was a fierce, determined look that screamed, "GET ME OUT OF HERE!!!"

"Get that child," I told Arleen.

Bringing Ana home did not save her from trouble. She was angry, unsettled, impossible to manage at school (and at home too, truth be told), and also wonderfully creative and endearingly quirky. Everyone fretted about Ana, and everyone cheered for her to persevere.

Despite her unruliness, Ana was remarkably self aware. She could work through things and was capable of growing surprisingly fast when circumstances challenged her. Although, or perhaps because, she began to smoke cigarettes when she was a junior in high school, she understood the danger of addiction. Despite her struggles, she managed to untangle herself from toxic friendships and stay away from drugs and alcohol.

When Ana came home to us, there were no dogs in the house. Eventually Arleen surprised us with a miniature English poodle puppy, Antoine. A few years later, still loopy from the anesthetic after a root canal, Arleen stopped into a pet store, not intending to make a purchase, and surprised us again with Isabella, another miniature English poodle.

Ana latched onto Isabella and wouldn't let go. She carried the little six-pound dog everywhere. But Isabella was Arleen's dog. One summer, when Ana was about fifteen, I stayed home with the children while Arleen took Isabella on a trip to visit old friends. Ana came unglued, freaking out with abandonment terror. I resolved that she should have a dog of her own, a bigger dog, better suited than Isabella to contend with Ana's energy.

Ana and Isabella

I looked at lots of dogs on lots of websites. There were a few who looked like candidates, but the adoption fees were more than I could manage, typically $200 to $400, or they were too far away, or they were already gone when I called. For a couple of weeks I kept looking, without success.

Then one day, on the New Haven Animal Shelter's website, I saw a dog whose picture spoke to me as clearly as Ana's had.

"Max: male, 4 - 5 years old, 26 pounds, Bichon/terrier mix." The animal control squad had found Max, alone and afraid, in a city park. No collar, fur overgrown and matted, but there was a microchip. Following up the information on the chip, Max's previous owners could not be found. But from the chip, they did know his name was Max.

I prayed, "God, please let us have this dog." I made the call. He was still available, and the adoption fee was $35. But there were forms to fill out, and there was competition. Others wanted Max too. The shelter would have to decide we were the best family for him. We would need to bring Antoine and Isabella to meet Max and show they would get along. It wasn't a done deal.

We piled in the minivan, Ana, her sisters, Antoine, Isabella, Arleen and me, and drove to New Haven to meet Max. We waited. Finally, a uniformed woman brought Max to the fenced area where dogs and their new families get introduced. I watched, tears in my eyes, as he went directly to Ana. As they played, it seemed they understood they were destined to be together. After both had been so traumatized by separation, they rejoiced in the newfound connection.

Then the officer asked us to bring Antoine and Isabella.

Antoine was fine, a true little gentleman, but Isabella seemed a little jealous of this new dog who was getting so much attention. "Not sure about that little dog," the officer said. I explained that Max would be Ana's dog, and Isabella was Arleen's dog. They would sleep in different rooms, and it was a big house. "We'll let you know," the officer said.

That night, I didn't sleep. The thought of losing Max was unbearable. What could I do? I went to my computer and wrote a letter to the shelter. I told Ana's story, how much she needed a friend. I promised that Max would have a good life with us, that Ana and the whole family would adore him. The next three days and nights, I couldn't rest. I knew I'd done all I could, but waiting was torture.

Finally, the call came. Yes, we could have Max.

A week later, on November 13, 2013, I wrote:

"Please accept our heartfelt thanks for making it possible to bring home Max. Everyone adores him, and especially, Ana's SO happy to have such a devoted friend to play with and keep her company. Max is magic. He's incredibly gentle, lots of fun, loves to cuddle, gets along beautifully with Antoine and Isabella. He's a wonderful, sweet soul who's miraculously appeared, to bless this family and especially this child who so very much has needed a friend like Max. We are profoundly grateful to you for having brought Max into our lives."

I tell people, Max is a rescue dog. But the truth is, we didn't rescue Max. He rescued us.

Max on Ana's bed

Ana graduated in 2015. High school was a rough passage, even with Max on hand for the home stretch, but she did graduate. She decided to move away from here, back near the place in northern New York where we'd lived before, where some of her older sisters had settled. She wanted a fresh start, with new friends, new opportunities.

She grieved over being separated from Max, but her life was too unsettled to take care of a dog. I worried and watched to see how she would adapt to life away from Max.

She moved around a bit, from one shared apartment to another, and from job to job. I watched as she began to get her bearings. Eventually she found a job she was perfectly suited to, at a garden center/pet supply store. People bring their dogs, and Ana, at the front counter, is the one who greets them and dispenses the treats.

She did adapt to life away from Max. She more than adapted, she blossomed. From an unruly, defiant, unmanageable student, she became a steady, responsible, valued employee and a treasured friend. I observed, Ana was able to bond with any dog, and it seemed, at least now that she was becoming more established, more secure in the world, she didn't need her own dog. At this new stage in her life, Ana just needed to be *around* dogs, and she'd found a way to do it.

And of course, I wondered how Max would adapt to Ana's being gone. For a week or so he seemed disoriented, but then he settled into a new pattern of connections. He figured out all the beds – which ones are occupied when. He figured out who likes to snuggle, who likes to give tummy rubs, who gives treats.

The thing I've observed about dogs is, they are instinctively able to ingratiate themselves with every human they have access to. They are geniuses at conveying, "You are the most important person in the world. I love you," not just to a single person, but to EVERYONE they encounter. It's a brilliant strategy. Make everyone love you and then, if someone goes away, there will still be plenty of people to feed you, snuggle with you and give you tummy rubs.

What follows is a sort of random, unintentional diary of life in this household, of my life. It begins while Ana was here, but mostly it's about the time after she had gone, after Max moved out of Ana's room and took over the house. There isn't much structure. There's a storyline of sorts, but it would be hard to sum up in a tidy sentence. Maybe it's like impressionistic art or like a mosaic, where the brushstrokes or the bits of colored glass seem random until you stand back. Then, when you begin to see how the pieces fit together, you see that something meaningful has been portrayed. Something beautiful, perhaps even something profound. This artwork, though, was not intentional, at least not intentional on my part. But it does portray something. Together, let's see if we can figure out what it means.

"Max," I said, "I wrote a book, and YOU'RE in it!
You're going to be famous."
"I thought I already WAS famous."
"Sorry. I should have said,
you're going to be FAMOUSER."

Angels, Beggars *and* Castaway Things

A Forager's Journey Home

I'm starting with the first entries after Max came to us, while Ana was still here. He was with her most of the time then, so he only pops in occasionally at first. Later on, as you'll see, he's around a lot more. Here and there you'll find a few re-posted flashbacks from earlier years, which I've kept whenever they seemed to fit.

2013

Nov 17, 2013 10:08am

Lesson from a large, green insect ...

Arleen and I came home one cold evening a couple of weeks ago. "Don't step there!" She said. I looked down, and saw a praying mantis, on her side, but alive. I put my hand down and she climbed onto it. "She would have died tonight, I think. It's going to freeze."

I set her up in an enclosure, went to the pet store, which was still open, and bought some crickets for her to eat. Did a little research and learned that mantises don't inevitably die after laying their eggs, can live a long time if it is warm enough.

So Princess, as Arleen has named her, lives with us now. She doesn't eat every day, isn't much trouble to care for. But I was thinking, if she survives 'til spring, as I hope, she'll be confined for a long time, nothing to do but wait for crickets, wait for spring.

And then it occurred to me. She doesn't mind. It's her nature to wait. She experiences time in a completely different way, feels no urgency, no sense that time can be lost or wasted.

Thank you for showing me that, Princess.

Nov 25, 2013 11:11am

dog (dôg), noun.

A voice-activated, self-propelled apparatus for determining the exact center of any bed.

Dec 07, 2013 8:07pm

Every now and then, during a spell that's difficult for whatever reason, I get a message like this from someone I've sent a whistle to:

"Hi Jerry

It arrived on Friday 5th, thank you so much, I am delighted with it. Beautiful tone from it. Well done and God bless your hands.

Merry Christmas to you and your family."

Note: As you read on, you'll find more about my work with these instruments, commonly called "tin whistles," "penny whistles," "Irish whistles" or simply "whistles." At the end of the book, I've included more detail in case you're interested.

Dec 09, 2013 11:01am

Completed 48 whistles yesterday. Still about two hundred whistles behind.

Dec 10, 2013 7:33am

Completed 28 whistles yesterday.

Dec 12, 2013 11:36pm

Student: "What is the nature of discipline?"
Teacher: "A disciplined person eats when he is hungry and rests when he is tired."

Dec 26, 2013 10:16am

When we may be thinking about New Year's resolutions, this came to mind. Jeff Applewhite posted it awhile back, and I thought it worth saving:

"Just for a minute wherever you are in the world and whatever you may be doing, I want you to try something. Stop. Just stop. And realize how utterly perfect you are just as you are. Let it wash over you.

Now see yourself in the court of unconditional love as the charges you have brought against yourself are dismissed. One by one. 'Not Guilty"... "Not Guilty"... feel the peace that surrounds and engulfs you.

And now take a good look at the prosecutor who read off the long list of charges against you. Look familiar? That's right, it should. It's you.

Now look at the kindly judge who just dismissed all the charges. He doesn't care what unkind things you did. He doesn't care who you hurt. He knows the game is set up this way. Nobody gets out perfect. He knows that what 'you do' cannot and never will touch the pure, loving, essence that 'you are.' Look closely. That's right. He's you also."

Dec 26, 2013 11:20am

Please consider this ...

In reaching out, anyone who extends their hand to help or offer a gift has made themselves vulnerable. When you accept their offering with sincere appreciation you validate the offerer, and receiving becomes itself something we can give. By acknowledging that we need what another has to give, and in a sense that we are incomplete without the other, we offer ourselves to them. What greater gift have we to offer than ourselves, and how simple a gift to give. We need only say the words, "Thank you."

Dec 28, 2013 11:26pm

In winter, the recycling center down the road is open Saturdays only, 'til 3:00. John, who runs the place, sets aside items he thinks people might be able to use. This summer, I picked up a nice lawn mower there that only needed some clean gas and a carburetor I already had. A nice RED lawnmower.

Today I towed my homemade utility trailer, on which I'd piled old bicycle skeletons from all the years I've cobbled bikes together for the children, along with a few other random metal things. As I tossed the bike frames

into the dumpster, I noticed John had set aside an old benchtop drill press. Solid, good heavy castings. The kind they mean when they say, "They don't make 'em like they used to."

I tore down the drill press, pulled out the bearings and ordered new, plus a new chuck. It needs a motor, which I'll select from the binful I collected from my Amish neighbors back in rural New York. The Amish community caught on to the fact that I like electric motors. Every now and then, a horse carriage would appear at our place and a soft-spoken, bearded gent would call me over and say, "Reuben Hershberger told me you might could use this motor, so I brought it for you if you're interested."

The drill press has a stamped copper plate that says, "Sears, Roebuck and Co. model 101.03582." There's a decal on the front that says "Superior Ball Bearings," "Modern Equipment" and a logo that's worn beyond recognition. I Googled the model number and learned it was made in the late thirties or early forties.

Lord, I love old machines.

2014

Jan 02, 2014 11:15am

"It is foolish to think we will enter heaven without entering into ourselves." "May you trust God that you are exactly where you are meant to be." "It is love alone that gives worth to all things."

~ *Teresa of Avila*

Jan 09, 2014 8:00am

Hello from Ana's room

Jan 14, 2014 4:53pm

Today Joe, the postal clerk, made a mistake processing one of the packages I was mailing and had to start over. I had been chattering as he worked and apologized for distracting him. "You didn't make me do that," he said. "No need to apologize."

"Well," I said, "keep the apology anyway, in case someone owes you one."

Driving home, I thought about this. It seems like a good idea, perhaps a useful thought exercise at minimum, and maybe more than that.

So here:

On behalf of anyone who has offended, hurt or wronged you in any way, who hasn't for whatever reason offered an apology, I apologize.

Jan 20, 2014 10:20am

"Construction of a solar air-heating collector using a flow through screen absorber" (builditsolar.com)

Finished assembling a workbench, 4 feet by 28 feet, on which I will construct two solar collectors, each 3 feet by 27 feet according to this design:

http://www.builditsolar.com/Experimental/AirColTesting/ScreenCollector/Building.htm

On sunny days, the two installed collectors will provide 32,000 BTU/hr of free heat.

Feb 07, 2014 9:58pm

It's a great day.

After nearly six years, I've finally finished setting up my 3 HP 240V 10-inch table saw that served me so well back in rural New York. It sat on my utility trailer under a tarp and I was afraid the elements had damaged the motor bearings. As it happened, I only had to replace the starter switch and it's good as ever.

Mar 01, 2014 9:01am

Excerpts from "The Dalai Lama's Ski Trip," Slate.com

The Dalai Lama arrived in Santa Fe on April 1, 1991. I was by his side every day from 6 a.m. until late in the evening. Traveling with him was an adventure. He was cheerful and full of enthusiasm – making quips, laughing, asking questions, rubbing his shaved head, and joking about his bad English. He did in fact stop and talk to anyone, no matter how many people were trying to rush him to his next appointment. When he spoke to you, it was as if he shut out the rest of the world to focus his entire sympathy, attention, care, and interest on you.

[After dinner] a young waitress with tangled, dirty-blond hair and a beaded headband began clearing our table. She stopped to listen to the conversation and finally sat down, abandoning her work. After a while, when there was a pause, she spoke to the Dalai Lama. "You didn't like your cookie?"

"Not hungry, thank you."

"Can I, um, ask a question?"

"Please."

She spoke with complete seriousness. "What is the meaning of life?"

In my entire week with the Dalai Lama, every conceivable question had been asked – except this one. People had been afraid to ask the one – the really big – question. There was a brief, stunned silence at the table.

The Dalai Lama answered immediately. "The meaning of life is happiness." He raised his finger, leaning forward, focusing on her as if she were the only person in the world. "Hard question is not, 'What is meaning of life?' That is easy question to answer! No, hard question is what make happiness. Money? Big house? Accomplishment? Friends? Or ..." He paused. "Compassion and good heart? This is question all human beings must try to answer: What make true happiness?" He gave this last question a peculiar emphasis and then fell silent, gazing at her with a smile.

"Thank you," she said, "thank you."

~ *Douglas Preston*

Apr 27, 2014 10:53pm

The Self is hidden in the lotus of the heart. Those who see themselves in all creatures go day by day into the world of Brahman hidden in the heart. Established in peace, they rise above body-consciousness to the supreme light of the Self. Immortal, free from fear, this Self is Brahman, called the True. Beyond the mortal and the immortal, he binds both worlds together. Those who know this live day after day in heaven in this very life.

~ *Chandogya Upanishad*

Apr 27, 2014 11:04pm

Keegan Loesel in 2011, playing his Freeman key of D Mellow Dog

Just returned from the Comhaltas Ceoltóirí Éireann (Irish Arts Association) Mid-Atlantic Convention and Fleadh (competition) in Parsippany, NJ.

I was told of two children who qualified to compete in All-Ireland (that's the world championship) playing my whistles in this weekend's competitions.

The mother of one of them, Keegan Loesel, told me, he looked around and saw every other player in his age group was playing a whistle by the same highly respected maker. Keegan said, "I don't care. I love my Mellow Dog, and I'm playing it in the Fleadh." He took second place and is on his way to Ireland. The other boy had lost his whistle, which was an inexpensive mass produced one, so his mother bought him a Freeman-tweaked Generation. Playing it an hour later, he won second in his own age group.

Note: I learned later, the 2014 under 12 All-Ireland Whistle Championship was won by Iarla McMahan, age 10. He played a Freeman-tweaked Bluebird. His mother told me, "The adjudicators commented how sweet the whistle sounded." Iarla went on to win the 2016 under 12 All-Ireland Uilleann Pipes Championship. Keegan went on to win the 2017 All-Ireland 15-18 Uilleann Pipes Slow Airs Championship.

Keegan in Ireland, August 2017,
practicing for his championship performance

May 21, 2014 5:28pm

We're putting in a vegetable garden for the first time on this property. Yesterday I borrowed Jim's tractor and plowed an area maybe 20 by 30 feet.

Jun 01, 2014 5:33pm

The garden plot is ready.

When digging postholes I hauled granite stones out of the ground, many of which were flat. The gate I built would have to swing out toward an uphill slope, which meant I had to dig out a level area the four-foot-wide gate could swing over. This, I paved with the flagstones. Very inviting effect.

When you build a bluebird box, you have to do it correctly. The dimensions have to be correct, the entrance hole has to be the right size, the box has to be placed correctly. You know you've built the bluebird box correctly only when a bluebird alights and decides to nest there.

Arleen is my bluebird. She loves her new garden.

Jun 03, 2014 8:47pm

The eye is not very sore after the surgery, but there are three sutures that stick out and poke the inside of my eyelid. It feels like I now have a tiny porcupine instead of an eyeball. I can't close my eyes to meditate, and I can't sleep comfortably for very long. The sutures will eventually dissolve, but it may be an interesting few weeks in the meantime.

Jun 11, 2014 3:13pm

Jessica Eaves from Guthrie, Oklahoma recently had her wallet stolen by a man while she was grocery shopping. Most people in that situation would immediately get the authorities involved, but she found a way to resolve her problem herself.

"I saw this gentleman down the aisle from me," Jessica tells us. "He walked behind me, and when I got a couple of aisles over, I realized my wallet was gone."

"I spotted him in a crowded aisle and approached him," she continues. "I'm a pretty out-there personality, but I was quiet and calm."

"I said to him, 'I think you have something of mine. I'm gonna give you a choice. You can either give me my wallet and I'll forgive you right now, and I'll even take you to the front and pay for your groceries."

The alternative? Jessica reporting him to the police.

"He reached into his hoodie pocket and gave me my wallet," she recalls, adding that the man was extremely grateful for her help and forgiveness.

"He started crying when we walked up to the front," she says. "He said he was sorry about 20 times by the time we went from the pickle aisle to the front. He told me he was desperate."

She spent $27 on his groceries, which included milk, bread, bologna, crackers, soup and cheese. "The last thing he said was, 'I'll never forget tonight. I'm broke, I have kids, I'm embarrassed and I'm sorry.'"

"Some people are critical because I didn't turn him in, but sometimes all you need is a second chance," says Jessica.

She adds, "My brother and I lost my dad to suicide when I was seven, and I remember him telling me years ago that no matter what I become in life, to always, always be kind."

~ *Yahoo News*

Jun 15, 2014 7:03pm

Yesterday, for the first time in a year, I was able to use my right eye for close work. Still somewhat blurry after the surgery two weeks ago, but this is nonetheless a very big deal.

Jun 18, 2014 2:13pm

Antoine's and Max's lookout post

Jun 19, 2014 11:45am

OK, so a week or so ago, I bought Arleen a little refrigerator for her birthday so she doesn't have to go all the way down to the kitchen when she wants something, and so the children won't steal her treats.

The next day, she said, "I may not be able to keep the refrigerator. It makes a high-pitched sound that's bothering me."

I went to the refrigerator and saw she had placed an orange index card on top, on which she'd written "F#?"

Listening, I determined there were some sympathetic vibrations in the sheet metal and tubing that were the source of the high-pitched sounds.

I had recently disposed of the previous little refrigerator, which had stopped working awhile back, and I had kept the magnetic strips from the door gaskets. I cut several pieces of magnetic strip and stuck them inside the sheet metal where it had been vibrating, on the assumption that increasing the mass of that surface would make it no longer resonate.

I was correct but there was still a high-pitched sound coming from the metal tubing near the compressor, which went away when I put a finger on the tubing. Hmmm ... How could I fasten something to that tube to make it heavier, that wouldn't rattle, without insulating so it wouldn't radiate heat properly?

Aha! I cut a length of soft solder, which was easy to wrap tightly around the tubing. It took some adjusting to eliminate the vibration, but I succeeded. The refrigerator now purrs quietly just as a proper refrigerator should. No annoying stray sounds.

I've revoiced thousands of penny whistles, but that's the first time I've revoiced a refrigerator.

Jun 20, 2014 7:07pm

OK, so I go down to the basement to do some whistle work in my machine shop, and there's water on the floor.

I know what's going on because the same thing happened a couple of times last winter. But I didn't want to work on the heating system until it was warm enough not to be a problem if the boiler was down awhile, in case I ran into something that took a long time to fix.

I throw away some unneeded stuff that had gotten wet or was in the way and start shoveling up water. If the puddles are deep enough, you can pick up water faster with a square shovel than with a mop.

I hear Natasha and Maria come into the house with their friend Brianna, returning from a sleepover at another friend's house. I go upstairs and tell Arleen and the girls I need someone to help mop up the water while I close down the system and recharge the air in the overflow tank.

Natasha starts mopping with the one mop we own, while Maria and Brianna move stuff out of the areas that are wet.

I work on the overflow tank awhile. Out of the corner of my eye, I see Arleen coming in the double doors (it's a walkout basement). She has a big commercial yellow bucket with wheels and a wringer, and a big string mop to complete the set. She tells me she walked over to Joe's house down the street and rolled it home.

I bring the mop/bucket/wringer set into the house and wheel it over where the girls are working. I start to mop a little to try it out. Natasha, who is twelve, says, "I want to do it! I've wanted to use one of those my WHOLE LIFE!"

Later, after I've finished working on the heating system, I come back around to where the girls are working. The mop bucket is almost full, so I offer to take it outside and dump it for them. When I return with the bucket, Brianna and Natasha start squabbling about who gets to use the mop. I tell them, "Work together nicely, girls."

It is impossible not to love these children.

Jun 25, 2014 12:43pm

We're out of heating oil. Ran out of hot water an hour ago. Orders are behind schedule because of time lost recovering from surgery. A customer wrote, "Keep your promises!" Felt discouraged.

Oh, well. Carry on. Just finished the first whistle order of the day. Tried the whistle. A little shrill in the upper register. Made the relevant adjustment. Tried the whistle. Wow. That's really good.

Feeling better now.

Jun 27, 2014 3:12pm

I saw Arleen drive off earlier today. After a short time, she returned. "Where did you go?" I asked. She said, "I went to the library and got some fish."

I don't know how she does it.

Jul 05, 2014 8:19am

I looked out the window this morning down toward the garden from an upstairs view. There are four by four posts around the perimeter, on which deer netting is hung up to seven feet. Nine of the posts are eight feet tall. The tenth, nearest the house, I never shortened. It's still its original height, about ten feet.

This morning, I looked out and saw a fuzzy blob on top of the tall post. Went and got my distance glasses and looked again. Some sort of bird. Not an owl. Bigger than a crow. Had a plump, downy belly, couldn't see its tail. Goofy, dumpy looking bird with its round, disheveled, gray belly the most prominent feature.

It seemed in no particular hurry. Sat a long time, turning its head, looking. A robin alighted on the next post, flitted its wings and chirped. After a minute or so of this, the larger bird flew off to the left, toward the ground below the deck.

In flight, magnificent. Powerful, four-foot wingspan. Red-tailed hawk, which we have lots of, but I'd never seen one so close. I looked directly down on its massive back as it glided below me just fifteen feet away. Wow.

Jul 12, 2014 6:45pm

I ran out of corrugated cardboard, which I use for mailing. The recycling center is open today until 3:00, so after the day's whistles were put out for the mail truck, I went over to get more.

Checked with John, the attendant, to make sure it would be OK to take the cardboard. Noticed quite a lot of interesting stuff where they leave things that might still have some use. He said, "Take as much as you want."

OK.

Two VERY nice bicycles, one an old-school ten-speed, the other a kid's size springtail mountain bike. Both in excellent shape, maybe needing an inner tube. There was a third bike, but there was more rust on it, and I didn't think it was the type the girls wanted, so I left it. Ana had especially mentioned she wants a bicycle. I've put quite a few together for the girls over the years, but I didn't have any in working order just now.

I loaded my loot and drove home. Arleen was about to leave with the girls to go shopping and had just come into the garage. I whispered, "Come over here." Showed her the two bikes. She said, "That's not the kind Ana wants. She wants the kind with the things sticking out the axles where people can ride along."

That would be the bike I left behind. It was five minutes of three. I scooted out of the driveway, got to the recycling center with two minutes to spare. Put the bike in the trunk and headed home.

When I got the bike out, I saw it's actually quite nice, in good shape except for rust on the axle pegs. Went over it and found it needed the brake pads positioned properly, a new front brake cable, which I had on hand, air in the tires, and apparently nothing else.

I brought it to the driveway to try out and the rear hub wouldn't engage. The pedals just spun. Brought it back into my shop, sprayed it with lubricant, but to no effect. Went to the computer and read up on BMX freewheel hub troubleshooting. Went back down to the shop, got nowhere and decided I'd have to take the hub off and replace it.

I didn't have the correct tools for this, so I rigged a clamp and tried loosening the threaded ring with a hammer and punch. It didn't budge. But after a few tries, I thought I heard a ratcheting sound when the wheel spun. Sure enough, the hammering had freed the pawls inside the hub and it started working.

Brought the bike back to the driveway and tried it again. Perfect!

Went and got Ana and showed her the bike. “Cool,” she said coolly. Ana’s going through the seventeen-year-old “too cool for school” stage. It isn’t cool to admit to a parental unit that you’re excited about anything they show you.

She tried it out. I went back to work in my office. A little later, she came around and said, “Do you have any black spray paint?” “I might,” I said. “What do you want to do?” “I want to paint these rusty pegs.” I got the paint and sprayed the pegs for her. And the front sprocket, which had originally been black too.

“I’m going to clean it up, make it look nice,” she said. She went in the house and came out with cleaning supplies. I got some steel wool and showed her how to get rust off of chrome. When she was done, it had become quite a respectable looking bike.

“I’m going for a ride,” she said.

Half an hour later, she came back to my office. “That’s a great bike!” she said enthusiastically. “Thank you SO much!”

July 13, 2014 9:21am

Natasha: “Max gets so hyped up.”
Me: “He’s a dog. It’s very exciting to be a dog.”

Jul 14, 2014 8:33am

Starting Wednesday and through to the end, my whistles and I will be at Catskills Irish Arts Week in East Durham, New York.

Jul 16, 2014 8:34am

I'm racing to get enough done before driving later today for the last four days of Catskills Irish Arts Week. I've learned I sell the same amount whether I'm there four days or seven, so I've used the first part of the week for other work.

It's total magic, that gathering. All the ten or fifteen motels and resorts in the little hill village of East Durham, New York full of Irish session music till the wee hours. Concerts every evening with the world's greatest Irish players. Always a scary rush getting ready, and then a few days in heaven.

Jul 16, 2014 11:48am

Well, it looks like I'm not going to get enough done to hit the road today for Catskills Irish Arts Week. So I'll be heading down as early as possible tomorrow (Thursday).

Jul 20, 2014 9:56pm

(from four years ago)

In which FreemanWhistles meets Mary Bergin ...

I mentioned that I would be attending Catskills Irish Arts Week.

Upon checking into the Blackthorn Resort around noon on Monday, I discovered that Mary Bergin would be leading the session in the Blackthorn pub Monday evening. This seemed fortuitous. I'd never met Mary, and had been hoping for years to get a chance to have her try my whistles.

Uncertain how to approach her, I mentioned to the barkeeper, Rob, who happens to be a whistle player and purchased a tweaked D Generation from me shortly after I arrived (which also seemed fortuitous), that I was unsure how to proceed. He said, "I know Mary. I've taken her class. When she arrives for the session, I'll tell her you're here."

Shortly before ten, Rob came around to where I was working on my laptop in the lobby and reported he'd seen Mary, told her about me, and she wanted to meet. So I went into the pub, which was packed of course, and found a place on the periphery up against the bar where I could observe the proceedings and wait for the room to clear out, which I understood would take some hours.

After a little while, a dog wandered through. A medium sized CALICO dog, the only such dog I've ever seen, with white, apricot and black fur, one blue eye and one brown eye. Seemed very much at home, friendly but polite, perfectly calm. Went around checking the place and the people out systematically, solicitously making sure each person was OK, until Rob the bartender came through, found the owner and explained the dog would have to be on a leash.

The owner leashed the dog, who remained perfectly well-mannered, and set himself and the dog up at the bar right next to me. As the evening proceeded, I engaged the owner in conversation, discovered he had no experience with Irish music and was feeling despondent because the human race is about to end. I made my best effort at offering reasons to look a little more on the bright side, but he would have none of it. The whole (long) time, I kept my eye on Mary to make sure I didn't miss an opportunity to make contact. However, the room remained quite full, and Mary's attention was clearly 100% occupied leading the session.

So I waited.

The room began to thin somewhat, and it began to look like my chance might come eventually.

Then the man turned to me and said, "I have to go to the bathroom. Would you mind taking the leash until I get back?" I did so, and the dog and I waited patiently, though I had a vaguely uneasy feeling about the arrangement.

Still a fair while before midnight, Mary rather suddenly got up, and the people who had come with her also got up. They worked their way through the seated participants and headed in the direction of the door. Not a good sign, I thought, and what with the dog that had been entrusted to me, I couldn't go after her. I couldn't be angry at the dog, who was the most innocent creature you could imagine, but there I was, stuck with a dog that belonged to someone else, and no way to save the opportunity. I watched Mary round the end of the bar toward the door and disappear from sight. Oh, well. Maybe next year.

Then, as I continued to look after where Mary had gone, I watched as she rematerialized from around the end of the bar, strode the length of the room directly up to me and asked, "Are you the man with the whistles?" (She seemed not to notice the calico dog.)

I admitted that I was, and asked if she was coming back. "No," she said, "I'm exhausted," and she asked how we might arrange for her to get some whistles to try. At which point, I opened the bag I had brought and handed her eleven whistles. She looked astonished and delighted at the same time, as if someone had just handed her a pot of gold. We agreed that I should show up just before her class the next day, and she could let me know what she thought of them. Knowing she likes Generations, I had brought her a selection of tweaked Generations, plus Mellow Dogs in D and C.

When I did arrive, I found Mary and the class already seated and involved with their instruction. I went to Mary's side, concerned that I was interrupting the lesson. She noticed me and immediately said, "I LOVE the Bb and I LOVE the F. The F has just the kind of sound I like." (This was a tweaked high F Generation.) She pulled the whistles out of her bag, indicating that she would give them back. I told her she should keep the Bb and F, and she seemed genuinely surprised. I said, "You'll have to pay for the Bb, though. The price is half a minute of being able to hear you play it."

She played for more than half a minute. She played an entire, fairly lengthy tune, though now I can't tell you if it was a slow air or a reel. All I can tell you is it was the most gorgeous thing I've ever heard, not least of all because she was playing a whistle I had created. After thanking her for such beautiful playing, I excused myself as quickly as possible, not wanting to hold up the class. (As the week went on, I worried that I had imposed on the students, but later, one who had been there said they'd loved it and liked the tune so much they made her teach it to them.)

Based on the fact that she said she liked the sound of the high F, and the fact that she hadn't seemed impressed with the tweaked Generations in C, D or Eb, I thought she might be looking for something brighter and purer voiced. I put together some Blackbirds in Eb, D and C and intercepted her in the parking lot just before she arrived for another lesson. She took the whistles, and I watched as she walked toward little St. Mary's church where the class was held, holding the whistles in the air as if they were a bouquet of flowers.

I found her a day or so later, and she said she liked the Blackbirds and would like to try a few more of them to see if she could find exactly the ones she wanted. She said something that made me think she might prefer a subtle change from the setup I had given her, so I went back to where I was working and glued up four with the adjustment. I found her after those had been completed and told her what I'd done.

All this transpired over the week of the event, leading up to Saturday, the final day, on which there would be an Irish music festival from noon to seven in the evening. Mary would be performing at two. She came around to my vendor's table about 12:30 and said she'd like to spend some time going over the whistles with me after her performance, but not before because beforehand she wanted to keep her mind on the performance.

During the time before her performance, people came and went, tried out whistles, talked about whistles, purchased whistles. A woman came to the table, said she plays the clarinet and would like to take up the whistle. We discussed the fact that the clarinet is a cantankerous instrument that overblows to the twelfth, but a saxophone's fingering is similar to a whistle's. She told me the middle register of a clarinet fingers similarly to a saxophone. So I told her to pretend she was playing the middle register of a clarinet and gave her a Mellow Dog to try.

She came back in a few minutes (my vendor's table was set where I could send people to a place they could hear themselves over the performers) and said she wanted to get her friend who plays the whistle so her friend could try the Mellow Dog and advise her.

In a few more minutes, she showed up with Mary Bergin! I burst out laughing and said, "Is this your friend who plays the whistle?" She said, "No, I couldn't find my friend, but I ran into Mary, and she said she'd try it for me." Mary tried the Mellow Dog, said, "I would have this whistle," and went on her way. I completed the sale and shortly after, listened to an absolutely transcendent set of music, performed by the great Mary Bergin.

Some more time passed, and Mary appeared at my table again. We went through the whistles, and she picked a C Blackbird, two D Blackbirds and two Eb Blackbirds that she said were exactly what she wanted. I checked with my calipers, and found that all had been set up the same way, with the adjustment I had made for her. (All Blackbirds are now set up that way.)

As we went through the whistles Mary had picked out, people came and went, asking about whistles, trying whistles, asking Mary for advice about whistles, asking Mary to try whistles for them, purchasing whistles. She showed no sign of impatience, but rather, clearly was enjoying herself.

"I love all whistles," she said.

Jul 21, 2014 11:57pm

I need a recipe for pickles.

Arleen planted eleven pickle plants and they're taking over Connecticut.

Jul 24, 2014 1:41pm

So Arleen comes around where I'm working and says, "Don't forget, we have a pickling date."

Oh baby.

Jul 27, 2014 9:15pm

Arleen and I finally got around to our pickling date. A good start, I think. We put up eight pints of dill pickle spears and two pints of bread and butter pickles.

Now that we're up and running, hopefully we'll be able to keep up with those marauding cucumber vines. There will be lots of tomatoes and summer squash too, that will likely go into jars. Now I have to build storage so we'll have shelves enough for the season's canning.

Jul 28, 2014 9:34am

This morning, I looked out at the scene beyond my second floor window and saw the dead tree I'd cut the bittersweet loose from had blown down.

I'm amazed by how relentlessly resourceful bittersweet vines are.

You can see their tendrils reaching far out from whatever they've ascended, ready to capture anything they touch. They climb to the top of trees, overwhelm the foliage with their own blanket of leaves and eventually kill the tree. The dead trunk will continue to stand even after the base has rotted through because the bittersweet vines become thick and woody trunks themselves, propping it and serving as anchoring lines. This dead tree would have stood for many more years if I hadn't cut the bittersweet from its base.

Bittersweet vines lying on the ground will take root. When you pull them up, you find the rooted length of vine just under the ground may be ten, twenty or more feet long before you get to what looks like an original root.

Where bittersweet vines cross each other on or in the ground, they graft together so every bittersweet vine in the forest feeds every other bittersweet vine. You can cut them off in many places without severing their connection with the soil.

Jul 28, 2014 9:36am

This morning's harvest: five slicing tomatoes, three salad cucumbers, a pint of cherry tomatoes. There's lettuce in the window box garden on the deck. There'll be a nice salad today. For now, it appears we're caught up with the pickling cukes.

Jul 28, 2014 11:34pm

Mountain lion in our yard tonight. Apparently they're fairly common in northeast Connecticut. The children saw it, came and got me, but it was gone. They got a clear look, and from their description, I've no doubt it was a mountain lion.

Note: A few days later, our neighbor commented she'd seen a mountain lion, which confirmed the children's sighting.

Jul 29, 2014 11:06pm

We have to be careful with our little dogs on the deck, to make sure they stay close to their humans and under or near chairs, tables, etc. We never leave them on the deck alone. The red-tailed hawks routinely swoop down close, sizing up menu options.

Today, when Arleen, the girls and the dogs were all on the deck, Ana saw a large bird coming close. REALLY large bird. It made one pass, then turned back and came again even closer, flying directly toward Isabella, our six-pound English poodle, before pulling up and soaring off.

It was a pelican! Hungry looking pelican. Too far from the ocean to fish, so maybe looking for something else to eat.

Yesterday the girls saw a double rainbow. We could tell a rainbow was about to appear, and we waited for it, watched as it started on one side and then in two or three seconds flung its arc across the sky. A stunning display.

Yesterday they saw the shooting rainbow, last night they saw a shooting star and a mountain lion, and today they saw a pelican. Tomorrow, if my calculations are correct, there will be a unicorn in our yard, or perhaps it will be reclining comfortably on the deck, waiting for our girls to come out and charm it.

Aug 05, 2014 9:21am

I don't care for shoes, seldom wear them. This morning I would be working where I'd cut out some thorn bushes, and there would be stickers on the ground.

So with a sigh, I put on my shoes. Went out the door, collected the wheelbarrow and went to the area where I'd torn out bittersweet and grape vines. The trunks, some of which were impressively thick, I had cut into lengths that would fit our someday-to-be-installed fireplace insert. I figured there's quite a bit of firewood there, once properly dried.

Gathered up, the sticks produced one very full wheelbarrow load. Brought them back to the place I built for stacking firewood under the deck, which I enclosed so it stays dry.

As I was stacking the wood I had to fuss a bit with the way the sticks were arranged so the pile wouldn't fall over. At that point I remembered:

One, two, buckle my shoe
Three, four, open the door
Five, Six, pick up sticks
Seven, eight, lay them straight.

How many millions, or more likely billions, of times have we humans re-enacted this exact sequence? In the simplest and most obvious ways, we are one humanity.

<u>*Aug 07, 2014 7:37pm*</u>

From the upstairs window at my desk, I have a view of trees and ferns, blackberry thicket, little clearing under a leaning beech resurrected from the bittersweet vines, old fallen tree offering a shady seat, new sumac, black-eyed Susan, Queen Anne's lace.

All this, to a significant degree, I sculpted with my own hands and a little help from my neighbor Jim's borrowed tractor. It gives tremendous pleasure.

<u>*Aug 12, 2014 1:06pm*</u>

The cherry tomatoes are in full stride. A quart or more per day, so wonderfully sweet and flavorful, they almost taste like grapes. Great in salads, cooked in omelets, etc.

They're "Sun Gold" tomatoes, which I can recommend highly if you're looking for great, easy-to-grow garden tomatoes.

<u>*Aug 12, 2014 10:36pm*</u>

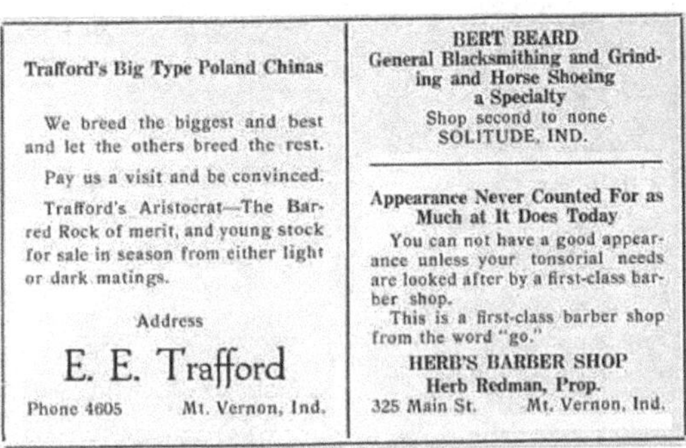

Trafford's Big Type Poland Chinas

We breed the biggest and best and let the others breed the rest.

Pay us a visit and be convinced.

Trafford's Aristocrat—The Barred Rock of merit, and young stock for sale in season from either light or dark matings.

Address

E. E. Trafford

Phone 4605 Mt. Vernon, Ind.

BERT BEARD
General Blacksmithing and Grinding and Horse Shoeing a Specialty
Shop second to none
SOLITUDE, IND.

Appearance Never Counted For as Much at It Does Today

You can not have a good appearance unless your tonsorial needs are looked after by a first-class barber shop.

This is a first-class barber shop from the word "go."

HERB'S BARBER SHOP
Herb Redman, Prop.
325 Main St. Mt. Vernon, Ind.

Newspaper ads from 1920 – Trafford would have been about forty

In the 1950's when I was little, my mother would take me to visit the stables of a noted horseman in Mount Vernon, Indiana by the name of E.E. Trafford. She told me this ...

One day Trafford was giving a woman a riding lesson. In the distance, thunderclouds were forming and it was clearly going to storm. The woman became concerned. She cut the lesson short, telling Trafford it looked like the storm would pass over her house shortly, and she would just have time to get home. She told him she'd left her pet monkey's cage outdoors, and he would panic if he were stranded in a thunderstorm.

As she hurried to her car, Trafford said, "That fool woman. If she wants kids, she should get married and have kids, instead of playing around with those silly pets." Just then, a horse came up to the fence where my mother and Trafford were standing, looking for attention. The old man stroked the horse's nose and said, "Hello, Son."

Aug 14, 2014 7:41pm

Earlier today, as I was working at my desk, Max came in, tail wagging, thrilled to see me, all snuggly and ingratiating. I noticed, he had an orange spot above his left eye that clearly was a residue of tomato sauce. How it got there without any getting on his mouth, I wondered.

I stopped what I was doing and got down to play with him for a minute. After a little of that, he stood up, raised his nose and sniffed the air to scout if there was any food in the room.

"I got nothin', Max," I said.

Instantly, he turned around and walked out.

Later, I learned about the orange residue. Ana had tossed Max a piece of rotini pasta, with sauce, from her bowl. Max still hasn't figured out how to catch.

Aug 15, 2014 3:18pm

Yesterday, it seems, Max managed to commandeer a whole Vidalia onion. Ate the entire thing, like an apple. Ana reports he insisted on sleeping right next to her as he usually does, breathing intensely onionated doggy breath into her face all night long.

The tomato sauce mark over his left eye is fading, gradually. The only food we've ever found Max won't eat is mushrooms.

Note: People commenting told me onions can be toxic for dogs. Searched online and found, it's rare, but can happen. I found many cases where people reported their dogs had eaten onions with no ill effects. We monitored Max carefully the next few days, but there were no signs of trouble.

Aug 24, 2014 9:10am

In a hurry to get on the road yesterday morning, I learned something new: You can't chew your breakfast and trim your whiskers at the same time.

Aug 25, 2014 11:05am

I had the pleasure this weekend of meeting and spending a little time with Kevin Rowsome at the Pipers' Gathering. What a gracious man he is.

As I sit here, I'm listening to his CD, "The Rowsome Tradition," on which he plays (among other instruments) a C# uilleann pipes set made *circa* 1898 by his great grandfather, William Rowsome.

Aug 25, 2014 8:46pm

Jim appeared this morning with his orange tractor, to mow some hay.

This evening before it began to get dark, as we sat on the deck we heard a spectacular chorus of coyotes close by. A little later, Natasha pointed out a red-tailed hawk sitting on the ground in the newly mown field. Shortly after, we watched a single coyote as she prowled the farthest portion of the hayfield, occasionally stopping to calmly exchange eye contact with us.

"In years of average population sizes, typical meadow vole population density is about 15 to 45 meadow voles per acre in old-field habitat. In peak years, their population densities may reach 150 per acre in marsh habitat (more favorable for meadow voles than old fields). Peak meadow vole abundance can exceed 1,482 meadow voles per acre in northern prairie wetlands." (Wikipedia)

Based on how often I see them, I would confidently say the meadow vole population in our hayfield exceeds 45 per acre, and I wouldn't be surprised if it actually approaches 150 per acre. Our hayfield borders protected marshes. I'm inclined to think they are fewer than 1,482 per acre, however.

In any case, the hawks and coyotes were delighted to see their dinner so much easier to access, thanks to the orange tractor that appeared this morning on their behalf.

Aug 26, 2014 12:00am

For me, the high point of this weekend's Pipers' Gathering was Joey Abarta's uilleann pipe performance during the Saturday night concert. Beautifully fluid and expressive playing, with masterful use of the regulators. Thank you, Joey.

Aug 26, 2014 8:26am

Since moving here in 2008, we haven't paid much attention to the fruit trees on the property. But this year, the Bosc and red Bartlett trees (one of each) produced an impressive crop. I hadn't looked at them for a week or two, was thinking those pears may be about ready to pick. Went out and saw the Bosc tree still heavily laden, but not a single Bartlett left. None on the ground either. What I did see, however, was that the tall grass around the tree was matted, the sign of deer having slept there. Breakfast in bed!

Sep 12, 2014 12:34pm

Driving to town for an errand yesterday, I saw the remains of a freshly demised possum at the edge of the road. Coming back, saw two largish birds (crows?) dining on the carrion. As I got closer, I could see they weren't crows. Bigger than crows. Silly, disheveled looking birds. They allowed me to come very close, sit in the car and watch awhile before they soared off on broad, powerful wings. Turkey vultures.

Sep 17, 2014 9:24am

"If I speak in the tongues of men and of angels, but have not love, I am a noisy gong or a clanging cymbal. And if I have prophetic powers, and understand all mysteries and all knowledge, and if I have all faith, so as to remove mountains, but have not love, I am nothing. If I give away all I have, and if I deliver up my body to be burned, but have not love, I gain nothing.

Love is patient and kind; love does not envy or boast; it is not arrogant or rude. It does not insist on its own way; it is not irritable or resentful; it does not rejoice at wrongdoing, but rejoices with the truth. Love bears all things, believes all things, hopes all things, endures all things.

Love never ends. As for prophecies, they will pass away; as for tongues, they will cease; as for knowledge, it will pass away. For we know in part and we prophesy in part, but when the perfect comes, the partial will pass away. When

I was a child, I spoke like a child, I thought like a child, I reasoned like a child. When I became a man, I gave up childish ways. For now we see in a mirror dimly, but then face to face. Now I know in part; then I shall know fully, even as I have been fully known.

So now faith, hope, and love abide, these three; but the greatest of these is love."

~ 1 Corinthians 13:1-13

Sep 21, 2014 11:26am

Wild turkeys in the yard. Max is barking his head off. The turkeys couldn't care less.

Oct 04, 2014 5:04pm

It is the highest of compliments when you run into your neighbor who farms and he says, "I've been admiring your tomato cages."

Note: They're made of wood, designed and built by me.

Oct 15, 2014 10:05pm

For some mysterious reason, suddenly we're up to our armpits in ladybugs.

Nov 03, 2014 10:31am

Max's front legs are too short and his body too long for standard doggy sitting. So instead he reclines majestically, as you see here.

Nov 04, 2014 10:03pm

My heartfelt gratitude to all of you who have chipped in to help us get through the situation my family is facing. Without you, this would have been a disaster. I will never forget what you've done. I've been able to keep the power, phone and Internet on, I've brought some of the bills current, and I've paid down part of a high-interest debt in a way that moved some of it to low interest, which will reduce the monthly bill. I still have a ways to go, however ...

You have my lifelong appreciation and thanks. You are treasure.

Nov 17, 2014 9:57pm

Ana was in a funk today because of some trouble with her schoolwork. This afternoon, she dyed her hair bright blue. That's cheered her up considerably.

2015

Jan 10, 2015 *10:34pm*

My father was a great storyteller (Written January 10, 2004, three weeks after he passed away, on my father's birthday) ...

He was a professional writer, started as a newspaper reporter, and he had a gift for seeing stories that others might miss.

Before WWII, he was reporting a political event where there was a long wait before the formalities.

As was his habit, he chatted up various of the people he encountered there, including a painter who was working on the premises. This was before the advent of paint rollers, and the painter was painting the walls of the place with a paintbrush. Back and forth, back and forth, into the bucket for more paint. Back and forth, back and forth, into the bucket for more paint.

He asked my father what kind of work he did. My father answered, "I'm a news reporter." The painter responded, "Isn't that kind of monotonous?"

Jan 16, 2015 9:06am

Are you going to give me that thing or what?

Jan 20, 2015 7:28pm

OK, so I'm on my way somewhere in the house. I walk past Mahlet and Natasha and I hear Mahlet saying "kissy face, kissy face, kissy face, kissy face, kissy face, kissy face ..."

I was puzzled, but I don't butt into their private conversations so I let it go. I did stop to tell them about the scary near miss I'd had earlier today with the alfalfa sprouts. (Arleen served alfalfa sprouts. This was problematic. I discovered, it's impossible to tell alfalfa sprouts from whiskers. My concern is, if I swallow my whiskers, I'll turn inside out. Natasha thought it was funny, Mahlet said, "I'm glad I don't have whiskers.")

As I start to walk away, I hear Mahlet again: "kissy face, kissy face, kissy face ..."

That was too much. I turned around and asked, "What are you doing?"

Mahlet showed me her iPod and said, "Look at Monica's pictures. She makes a kissy face EVERY TIME."

Jan 23, 2015 11:21pm

WHISTLE-TWEAKING BREAKTHROUGH could change the music world (seriously) with your help ...

Today I met with Drs. Richard Bass (music theory) and Sina Shahbazmohamadi (engineering) of the University of Connecticut Digital Musicology Group.

They, together with Dr. Robert Howe, are famous for using advanced CT imaging to create exact replicas of rare historic instruments, including saxophone mouthpieces made by Adolphe Sax himself. UConn is the only place in North America doing this. As it happens, the University of Connecticut is a short drive from my house.

Both gentlemen were extremely gracious and offered UConn's help to replicate the tweaked whistles I've spent the past ten years perfecting. CT scanning my tweaked whistleheads to create CAD computer files I can work with is the next step toward mass production, which has been my goal since I began this work.

I would like to put high quality, affordable whistles in every music store and Irish gift shop so EVERYONE'S first experience with the instrument is a fulfilling one.

I've heard the same story many times: Long ago, someone took an interest in Irish music, bought a whistle and began learning to play. After a short time, frustrated by the cantankerousness of the instrument and unsure whether the problem was their playing or the whistle itself, they gave up. People have told me, "If I'd gotten one of your whistles twenty years ago instead of the [name of brand] I did buy, I would have been playing twenty years by now.

Whistle teachers all over the world recommend my instruments. Every year, the Mid-Atlantic chapter of Comhaltas Ceoltóirí Éireann (Irish Arts Association) asks me to make my whistles available at their events so the students can get a good start (CCE organizes the Irish music and dance competitions worldwide that culminate in the All-Ireland Fleadh every year).

I'm proud to say Freeman-tweaked whistles are starting to show up at the All-Ireland Fleadh world championship competitions, played by students who started on them several years ago. I'm also proud to say there are now quite a few All-Ireland Champions who've performed or recorded with my instruments.

I believe getting my whistles into mass production and making them available everywhere will make a difference in how many people stay with the music and go on to become lifelong players.

That is a significant thing:

It will strengthen Irish music everywhere.

It will put more music in the world.

It will give more people the joy of making their own music.

That's the vision that's kept me going all these years, tweaking tens of thousands of whistles, one at a time, trudging along toward this goal.

Feb 04, 2015 10:27pm

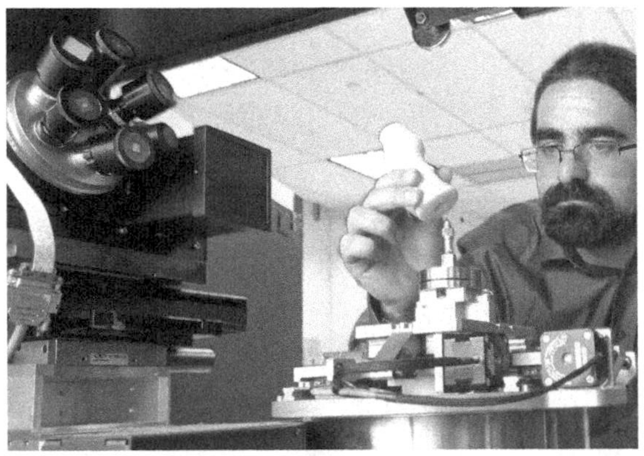

Peter Morenus/UConn

Sina Shahbazmohamadi, Ph.D. positions a musical instrument part in the ZEISS Xradia 510 Versa precision CT scanner

Today I opened a dedicated savings account for the whistle-imaging project, and I delivered a packet of prototype whistleheads to the University of Connecticut to be scanned on their precision CT machine.

I would have been happy with a resolution of 25 microns (.001 inches). At seven-tenths of a micron (.00003 inches), this machine at the University of Connecticut is thirty-five times higher resolution, one thirty-five thousandth of an inch. It's like someone offered to let me use the Hubble telescope!

Feb 05, 2015 4:14pm

Haiku by a fourth grader:

Five syllables here
Seven more syllables there
Are you happy now?

Mar 22, 2015 11:15pm

Drilled 396 holes this evening. Completed 66 alto A whistle tonebodies.

Mar 23, 2015 11:06am

Max 'n me, chillin'

Mar 24, 2015 5:48pm

A synchronicity of desperation ...

Ana's in her senior year at high school. A couple of days ago, she showed me a Subway gift card she'd gotten as an award for something at school.

"Subway food gives me headaches," she said. "There's ten dollars on here. If you give me five dollars, you can have it."

"OK," I said, "but I don't have any money. I can pay you when I get some cash."

Ana's been trying to quit smoking. She's tried cold turkey several times without success, but lately, she's been able to smoke fewer cigarettes by only bringing two or three to school with her. She isn't working, and she's always scraping for cigarette money. That would explain the urgency about five dollars.

There's a homeless guy I see sometimes near the grocery store. I bought him a hot Philly cheesesteak sandwich and half a gallon of chocolate milk a few weeks ago on a biting cold day, along with a black, zipper hoodie I picked up at the Salvation Army Store where I like to shop (that's where I got the paper shredder I gave my rats for Christmas).

I told Joe, the cashier I've become friendly with, I wanted the hoodie for a homeless guy, and he charged me $1.50 for it. As I drove off, I was chuckling to myself, "I'm connected, man. I know a guy at the Salvation Army Store, can get great deals on stuff." Driving back to my homeless guy, I turned the defroster all the way up and put the hoodie on the dashboard to warm it.

When Ana sold me the Subway card, I thought I might give it to that homeless guy, but his post is too far from a Subway shop. I'd have to drive him.

Today I had to go to the post office right next to the downtown Subway shop. I thought, "Better bring the gift card. Maybe I'll find something to do with it."

I parked in front of the Subway and carried my packages into the post office. Put them on the counter (I'd already processed them online) and walked out again.

As I turned to go up the block toward my car, I overtook a short, maybe fifty or so, olive-skinned man with wavy hair almost to his waist. As I passed him, he turned to me and said something unintelligible. I thought he seemed mentally ill and hurried on, hoping he wasn't aggressive. Then I remembered the Subway card.

I turned and walked back to him. Pulled the card out of my pocket and said, "Can you use this? It has ten dollars on it."

Instantly he started bawling, "I'm hungry. I'm HUNGRY!!! God bless you, God bless you, God bless you, God bless you, God bless you." He knelt on the pavement. I took his hand and gently pulled him back to his feet.

"C'mon, man. Let's get you a sandwich."

He continued to bawl and bless me as we walked toward the Subway shop. He pointed to the sky and shouted, "THANK YOU GOD!" I put my arm around him as we walked.

I opened the door to the Subway shop for him. He thanked me again and walked in. I drove off, wishing I could have done more.

Apr 01, 2015 2:47pm

Over the weekend, I got an email from one of the organizers of the New England Folk Festival (April 24-26, Mansfield, MA), asking if I would like to fill the last open position at the vendors' craft pavilion.

If any of you will be there, please come by and play a tune or two. I'm not a gifted player by any means, and it always helps when a competent musician comes along and plays my instruments for people to hear.

I'm optimistic about this. The events where my whistles fare best are those with a lot of teaching and session play, which the New England Folk Festival has in a big way.

I've been doing this long enough now to have seen an actual long-range effect in a music community. For example, the first person to play a Freeman whistle at the All-Ireland Championships began with a Mellow Dog his mother bought him when he was seven, at another music event eight years ago. [In 2017, that young man won the age 15-18 All-Ireland Championship for Uilleann Pipes Slow Airs.] By now, I've done around 20,000 Freeman-tweaked whistles.

This festival will be attended by several thousand folk music enthusiasts. I'm hoping enough bring my whistles home and play them in their sessions and performances, it will help sow some more seeds for the whistle in the American folk music community.

Apr 28, 2015 10:47pm

All-Ireland Championship won with Freeman Bluebird

I just learned, the 2014 All-Ireland age under-12 Whistle Championship was won by Iarla McMahon, 10, of County Down playing a Freeman-tweaked key of D Bluebird.

Keegan Loesel (age 15) competed in several 2014 All-Ireland categories on Freeman whistles. To my knowledge, Iarla's the first to win the top honor with one. [Keegan won the All-Ireland age 15-18 Uilleann Pipes Slow airs Championship in 2017.]

May 18, 2015 8:14pm

Labor-saving devices ...

Last year, when I first put in the garden, I borrowed the neighbor's tractor and auger attachment to dig the post holes. Because the ground is so rocky, I ended up with cone-shaped craters, not quite where I'd wanted them, which I had to fill back in around the posts. And despite the sophisticated technology, I had to dig many big rocks out of the ground with my bare hands.

I learned, among other things, that 15 by 22-1/2 foot garden isn't big enough.

So this year, I dug out all but four of the posts, which of course, I'd anchored in concrete, and quadrupled the size of the garden. That calls for eighteen new post holes; as of this evening, I've six more posts to set.

I decided to dispense with the tractor and power auger and bought a two-handled clamshell post-hole digger and six-foot steel bar. Day by day, as I've gotten the hang of these "primitive" tools, I've found the serious power tool is the steel bar, which has a chisel point on one end and a spike point on the other.

It took five or six post holes to figure out the spike end is the workhorse. It loosens the soil, finds the spaces between the rocks, wedges them apart, and can even split some of them. The clamshell post-hole digger I use mostly to remove loose dirt. The bar does all the work.

I can dig a nice post hole pretty fast, and most of the rocks come loose with reasonable effort. It's still hard work, but it's straightforward and efficient. So at least with the soil we have around here, seventy dollars worth of tools can dig better post holes faster and with less labor than thousands worth of machinery.

Jun 08, 2015 8:36pm

The sixteen tomato plants (eight Sun Gold, eight Brandywine) that waited patiently in their plastic pots on the deck while I brought 7,000 pounds of compost, fixed the lawn tractor, tilled, and put up chicken wire and deer net are finally in the garden. It's a beautiful day.

Jun 09, 2015 9:38am

Finally put in the ten pink rose bushes Arleen bought some weeks ago. They've waited along with an assortment of vegetable plants while I scrambled to get the garden plot ready. The roses make a row beside the garden for viewing from the deck.

Jun 24, 2015 3:48pm

I've finally caught up with the garden.

Today I finished the tomato cages, just as the plants were starting to fall over for lack of support.

Last year I built six, four-foot-tall cages, which we used for the Sun Gold cherry tomatoes. They were too small, so this year, I made two more four-foot-tall cages and bequeathed them to the eight Brandywine plants we put in this spring. They don't grow as tall.

I built eight new, five foot tall cages for the eight Sun Golds we put in this year. We'll see how they do.

The first part of the soaker watering system is in, five rows for the chard, cauliflower and broccoli. I'll add to the system for the tomatoes, cukes, squash and cantaloupe, but I'm ahead of the game on that. There's been plenty of rain, expected to continue through the rest of the week, so I won't need to water for awhile.

Jun 25, 2015 8:55pm

This has been a big week. I've learned two important, even transformative, life skills. I can hardly contain my excitement and I had to tell somebody:

1. I learned how to start wild black-eyed Susans from gathered seeds and get them to bloom the first year (they're biennial and normally only bloom the second year).

2. I've learned how to stretch a tight-fitting pair of shoes by filling the toe with a plastic bag full of water and putting them in the freezer overnight.

Wow. I hope I can get to sleep. The idea of those shoes in the freezer all night slowly stretching out so they don't pinch my toes any more could keep me awake for hours. It's just too much excitement.

Jun 26, 2015 12:57pm

Not having a great day.

There's minus $38.31 in my PayPal account, $6.08 in my checking account. I can't ship orders that should go out today because there's no money for postage. I've an important wholesale order to fill (for the Swannanoa Gathering) that I haven't been able to complete because my energy has collapsed the last few days. I keep having to give up and go back to bed. I'm running out of inventory to sell, but I can't order more until I get some cash flowing again.

I've mentioned now and then that I have Chronic Fatigue Syndrome. On the surface, I look fine. To most onlookers, this is completely invisible, but it limits my ability to get things done.

Thanks for listening.

Jul 11, 2015 7:41pm

Max got a haircut – Someone noted a resemblance

Jul 29, 2015 1:21pm

Yesterday, we were almost out of milk.

When I was out running some errands, I ran into Aldi's and bought a gallon. Put it in the refrigerator and noticed the small amount of milk that was still there when I left had been finished off while I was out.

Last night, I dreamed Arleen had picked up another gallon when she was dropping the children off at the library. This morning I was disappointed to look in the refrigerator and only see the gallon I'd picked up at Aldi's. To my surprise, my dream gallon of milk was not there.

Jul 31, 2015 8:10pm

Well, it turns out, deer can't climb trees after all.

There are two pear trees on the property that were here when we moved in. Last year was the first year one of them bore a lot of fruit. I'd been watching the pears ripen, getting ready to pick them. In a single night, deer ate all the pears off the tree, including the ones at the very top. It's a tall tree. Waaaaay far up to those topmost pears.

How'd the deer reach those highest branches? For the whole year, I've had cartoons running through my head of deer standing on top of deer, deer jumping up and down on their hind legs, deer climbing trees ...

Today I determined to pick the tree, early enough to beat the tree-climbing deer.

First, I mowed the tall grass underneath. Then I climbed a ladder and did some pruning. As I jostled the tree, pears began to rain down. From the ladder, I shook the top part of the tree. Every pear on those top limbs fell. When I got back to the ground, I shook the trunk. The rest of the pears fell. Every last pear was on the ground.

I went inside, told the girls about the pears and asked them to bring bags to gather them.

Now I know how the deer did it. They shook the tree.

Aug 07, 2015 11:34am

npr.org: "3-D Printers Bring Historic Instruments Back To The Future"

Here's an NPR story from May, 2015 about the University of Connecticut group that's helping me replicate my whistle designs. You can hear how original Adolphe Sax saxophone from the 1860's was supposed to sound:

http://www.npr.org/sections/deceptivecadence/2015/05/02/403273608/3-d-printers-bring-historic-instruments-back-to-the-future

Aug 10, 2015 8:24am

A friend pointed out what an amazing coincidence it is that I live near the only place in the country doing the type of precision 3D scanning I need to get my whistle designs ready for mass production.

I replied, "We moved here seven years ago for a job for Arleen that didn't work out. But it's a wonderful place to live, in an area where there are several important Irish music events. Very helpful to my work. And, as you said, it's next to the only place in North America that's doing this kind of imaging.

That tells me, while we only see one moment at a time, God sees all time and all things together and orchestrates past, present and future perfectly, effortlessly, automatically, even when we have no idea or plan at all."

Note: UConn's historic instrument 3D scanning project ended soon after they took the images of my whistleheads. It was such a short-lived program, it was almost as though they'd done it just for me.

Aug 13, 2015 8:18am

The 30-day crowdfunding campaign has concluded. We raised $5,975, which will fund the 3D scanning/modeling/prototyping part of the project with another $1,575 toward the tonebodies.

I'll need around $3,400 more to get a proper start on the brass tubing, and then there will be punch and die sets to build, so I'm keeping the crowdfunding page open for ongoing contributions.

Heartfelt thanks for all your encouragement and support. There's no way I could have financed the once-in-a-lifetime opportunity with the University of Connecticut to computerize these designs without your generous help.

The income from tweaking whistles has never been very much. As many of you know, I've struggled financially. But I've stayed with it because I have felt it was important for the future of the music, for the children coming along and the older folks approaching Irish traditional music for the first time.

I've always considered the tweaking work to be preliminary to mass production. Getting into mass production will change the economics of the business and should put things on a better footing.

I'm 62 years old and in excellent health overall. (I have lived with Chronic Fatigue Syndrome for over 20 years, but it is well-managed.) Not long ago, after losing some weight and suddenly feeling a lot younger, I realized I've probably another thirty years ahead of me.

In that time, I intend to create a body of work in the form of affordable, high-quality, widely available musical instruments that will continue to be produced long after I'm gone.

In addition to a complete line of "Generation-style" whistles in various keys and voicings, there are other designs I intend to develop, beautiful whistle voicings that aren't heard enough in the world. The 3D modeling and prototyping capabilities this project has helped with, will also facilitate that work.

Again, thank you so much for all your encouragement and support. You're a treasure, and I'm grateful for your friendship.

<u>*Aug 20, 2015 12:04pm*</u>

There's a problem with our Sun Gold cherry tomato plants

Now six or seven feet tall, the tomatoes are ripening so fast, by the time I finish picking them, more tomatoes have ripened and I have to go back and start over.

<u>*Sep 16, 2015 6:31pm*</u>

Ana came to visit
She wrote, "Miss him so much!"

<u>*Sep 26, 2015 8:01pm*</u>

About a week ago I picked the second pear tree (the one the deer didn't pick), a Bosc. It yielded about 20 gallons of fruit. The pears finished ripening and over the last two days we put up 31 quarts of pear butter (forty-one 24 oz. jars). There's nothing in the jars except pears, and it tastes amazing.

<u>*Sep 27, 2015 2:02pm*</u>

At the pharmacy today, I tried out their new automated blood pressure testing station. It was a harrowing experience.

I sat at the station and pushed the button. An authoritative voice said, "Place your arm in the cuff and sit quietly. When you are ready to begin the test, press the button."

I pushed the button again, and the cuff tightened around my arm. The voice instructed me to sit quietly throughout the test. Then it said, "When the test is completed, you will be asked to remove your arm."

<u>*Sep 28, w2015 1:11pm*</u>

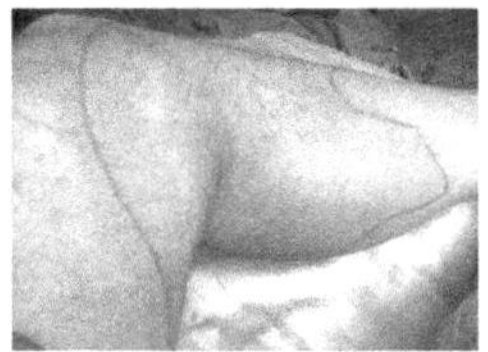

This, according to my doctor, is Lyme disease. The black outline is where Arleen and I traced the borders of the rash four days ago. Doxycyline, 100 mg BID for three weeks. Welcome to Connecticut, Mr. Freeman.

Note: After some reading, I concluded three weeks wasn't a long enough course of treatment. My doctor declined to prescribe more, so I found an online source for doxycycline and continued for another three weeks.

<u>*Oct 24, 2015 10:32am*</u>

Whistlemaker's anxiety dream ...

All I remember of the dream is commenting to someone trying a whistle: "That C-natural is noticeably sharp."

<u>*Oct 27, 2015 9:35pm*</u>

May there be peace in the heavens, peace in the atmosphere, peace on the earth. Let there be coolness in the water, healing in the herbs and peace radiating from the trees. Let there be harmony in the planets and in the stars, and perfection in eternal knowledge. May everything in the universe be at peace. Let peace pervade everywhere, at all times. May I experience that peace within my own heart.

~ *Yajur Veda 36.17*

<u>*Nov 2, 2015 4:28pm*</u>

Stupid human.

7:30 this morning: "Max, want to go OUT?"

Max jumps up, races to the stairs, looks back at me like, "C'mon, you idiot. YES I WANT TO GO OUT!!! What's the matter with you?"

I started to explain about Daylight Saving Time and why we set all the clocks back an hour last night but I realized, it's a REALLY dumb idea. You're right, Max. Humans ARE stupid.

<u>*Nov 19, 2015 1:19pm*</u>

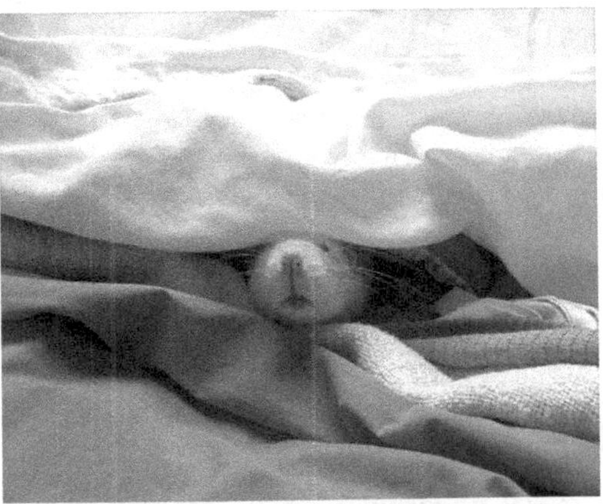

Here's Piglet, who was a key member of Global Pennywhistle Tweaking Research and Production Consortium Headquarters staff during an especially dynamic period. We owe much of our tremendous growth and progress to the resourcefulness and creativity of this remarkable rodent.

Nov 29, 2015 9:46pm

Here's the solar collector I started building last year.

Didn't finish in time for heating season and spent the summer on garden, etc. Now I'm back to work on it, hope to have it up and heating the house by Christmas.

It's 26 feet 10 inches long, 3 feet high. Sixteen thousand BTU per hour on a sunny day no matter how cold the outside air temperature.

Now I have to mount it on the south end of the house, build the duct work, install the fan, run the wiring and hook up the controls.

Dec 01, 2015 3:02pm

It's a great day ...

After sixty-three years, I've finally figured out how to eat a grapefruit.

Dec 04, 2015 7:22pm

Today I found a filling station nearby that sells B20 biodiesel (20% biodiesel, 80% petrodiesel).

Filled the tank. Bought a spare fuel filter in case the biodiesel cleans out the tank to the point that debris clogs the filter. They say you may go through a filter or two before everything's clean.

I've been wanting to run biodiesel in my 2000 VW TDI since the day I bought it. Eventually, I want to run both my car and the household heating boiler on B99 (99% biodiesel). I'll have to make some modifications to the burner (different nozzle, possibly different fire eye, etc.) before I can make the changeover, so today I ordered a delivery of B20 to heat the house.

Dec 09, 2015 4:16pm

So far, we've raised $358 to help Pandit Sharma repay the loan he took for medical treatment for his parents. We still have $242 to go to reach the total of $600 (40,000 Rupees) he has to repay before the end of the month.

Heartfelt thanks to all who have contributed so far.

Dec 11, 2015 2:15pm

"In Louisville, at the corner of Fourth and Walnut, in the center of the shopping district, I was suddenly overwhelmed with the realization that I loved all these people, that they were mine and I theirs, that we could not be alien to one another even though we were total strangers. It was like waking from a dream of separateness, of spurious self-isolation in a special world ...

This sense of liberation from an illusory difference was such a relief and such a joy to me that I almost laughed out loud ... I have the immense joy of being man, a member of a race in which God Himself became incarnate. As if the sorrows and stupidities of the human condition could overwhelm me, now that I realize what we all are. And if only everybody could realize this! But it cannot be explained. There is no way of telling people that they are all walking around shining like the sun.

Then it was as if I suddenly saw the secret beauty of their hearts, the depths of their hearts where neither sin nor desire nor self-knowledge can reach, the core of their reality, the person that each one is in God's eyes. If only they could all see themselves as they really are. If only we could see each other that way all the time. There would be no more war, no more hatred, no more cruelty, no more greed ... But this cannot be seen, only believed and 'understood' by a peculiar gift."

~ *Thomas Merton, Conjectures of a Guilty Bystander*

Dec 21, 2015 11:00pm

Richard Dalby wrote:

Taught Transcendental Meditation to a couple of recent Veterans of the wars in Iraq and Afghanistan over the weekend. They are both doing great. One said tonight, "this is the first time in 12 years I have been able to relax ..."

(Following is a synopsis not an exact quote): This is first time I feel like I'm not chasing something I can never reach. I did all the other meditations, where you are supposed to clear your mind, or guided meditations where you listen to someone or to recordings. I did CPT therapy. Nothing worked. In two days, with TM, I feel better than I have with years of therapy. In a way it makes me angry I wasted all those years on things that didn't work.

It's time for the VA to make this available to all veterans.

Dec 24, 2015 8:11am

Message this morning from Pandit Sharma: "Good morning Jerry ji. I picked money today and going pay back him his money ji. Thank you so much ji."

Again, deepest thanks to all who've contributed to help Panditji repay the loan he took for his parents' medical expenses.

Best wishes, and Merry Christmas

Dec 25, 2015 5:37pm

Hoisted the season's biggest Christmas ornament today

Now I have to install the fan, duct, wiring and controls. Hope it makes hot air!

2016

Jan 26, 2016 1:38pm

Scientifically tested (not) and proven effective (for me!)
Four-point weight management program:

1. Don't eat when I'm not hungry.
2. Avoid high-glycemic carbs and added sugars, eliminate snack foods.

3. Count calories.

4. Weigh daily.

I lost 20 pounds last spring with this approach. Gained seven pounds over the holidays. Got back on the program and I've lost four of the seven gained. Not to mention, I feel so much better when I eat this way.

Note: I've learned how many calories the various things I eat contain, don't need to count them nowadays. This system always works for me.

Jan 26, 2016 3:08pm

The most interesting dog in the world

"I don't always eat table scraps, but when I do, I prefer ... Wait a minute. I'll eat whatever you've got!"

Jan 30, 2016 7:36pm

I'm pleased to report, the solar collector does, in fact, make hot air.

I spent the last couple of weeks trying different ducting and fan arrangements, and I'm now satisfied with the result.

After checking the position of the collector relative to due south and the sun's angle from the horizon, I've revised the predicted heat output down to 10,000 - 12,000 BTU/hr. When it's running, it raises the air temperature three or four degrees and keeps the main heating boiler from coming on for several hours.

I must say, it's incredibly satisfying on a cold, sunny day to notice hot air blowing into the kitchen, a free gift from Nature.

Now I'm starting to build a second solar collector for the upstairs. It will be on the roof above the first collector. The available space also will allow it to be about 50% bigger. I project the heat output of the second collector will be about 22,000 - 24,000 BTU/hr.

I don't know if there will be enough time to complete the second collector before the end of heating season, but I enjoy working on it, so we'll see how far it gets. I've purchased most of the materials and enlarged the workbench. I'll be able to start working on it as soon as tomorrow.

Note: I still haven't begun. In the year and a half since this posting, however, I've improved the design and fixed my MIG welder so I can use steel instead of wood.

And, by the way, I now have a five-feet wide by thirty-two-feet long workbench in my basement.

Feb 01, 2016 11:16am

I can't find anything that isn't Grace.
The surrendering is Grace.
The struggling is also Grace.
And the little "me" that keeps you functioning in the universe,
that makes it possible for you to BE the Vastness
that ... is also Grace.

But then, accepting all that,
that's "surrendering to Grace," isn't it?
Sometimes we surrender to the fact that there is something to do;
and sometimes we surrender to the fact that there is nothing to do.

The mother surrenders to the labor of giving birth.
She doesn't surrender to silence in that moment, she surrenders to labor.
And then, when she sleeps with her newborn child, she surrenders to silence.

Feb 03, 2016 6:35pm

Hangin' out

Feb 24, 2016 7:07pm

I wonder if anyone knows, is there a setting on Facebook you can specify so someone can only post on your timeline when they're sober?

Mar 07, 2016 11:42pm

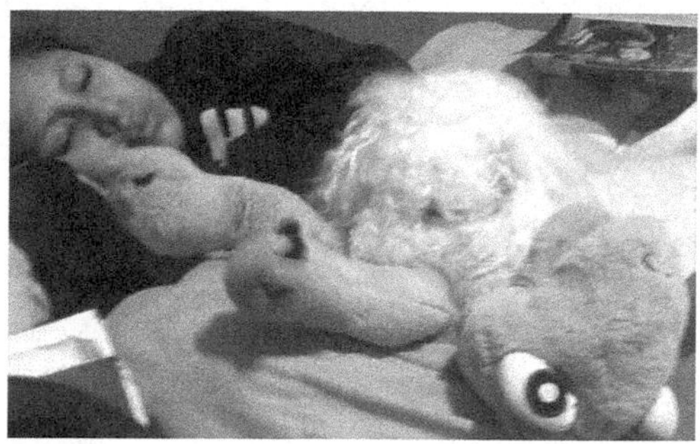

Maria, Max and Max's plush toy de jour

Mar 12, 2016 3:37pm

A couple of months ago, there was a nice-looking lawn tractor sitting next to the dumpster at the recycling transfer station around the corner. "Is that lawn tractor available?" I asked. "Yup," said Dan, the guy who runs the place (John has gone to work for another town). "Do you know what's wrong with it?" I asked. "The guy said it has a blown head gasket." It also had four flat tires and no battery.

I told him I'd be right back with my utility trailer. I went home, ran my air compressor until the tank filled with air and loaded it on the trailer.

When I got back, I found that the ramp I brought with my trailer was too narrow for the lawn tractor. So I looked around for an alternative. Beside the construction materials dumpster, to my amazement, were two, 12-foot, two by twelve scaffold planks. The tires were so bad, I had to keep refilling them as I wrestled the lawn tractor up onto the trailer.

As soon as I got home, I checked the tire sizes and ordered inner tubes. I paid about forty dollars total.

As it turns out, that model of lawn tractor has a one cylinder, 17.5 horsepower engine that's easy to work on. I cleaned up the engine, which was caked with grime from leaked oil.

I pulled the head and found the cylinder walls were perfect; you can still see honing marks from when it was manufactured. It never ran dry.

But the head was warped. Starting with 60-grit sandpaper taped to the milled surface of my table saw, I flattened the head by carefully honing it back and forth across the paper. I finished it with finer and finer paper down to 800 grit.

Then I lapped the valves and reassembled the engine with a new head gasket. Finished it all yesterday. I bought a new battery, and it started right up.

It ran rough, billowed white smoke, and I worried something else might be wrong. Sprayed in some carburetor cleaner and let the engine run. After several minutes, the smoke cleared and the engine smoothed out. Whew. It was just oil burning off, left over from the blown head gasket.

It runs like a champ. Like new.

Mar 21, 2016 10:43am

"It is true that we are called to wholeness. But the reality is that we can never be completely whole in and of ourselves. ... So we are called to wholeness and simultaneously to recognize our incompleteness; to power and to acknowledge our weakness; and to both individuation and to interdependence.

'Rugged' individualism ... runs with only one side of the paradox and incorporates only one half of our humanity. It recognizes that we are called to individuation, power and wholeness. But it denies entirely the other part of our story: that we can never fully get there and that we are, of necessity in our uniqueness, weak imperfect creatures who need each other.

This denial can be sustained only by pretense. ... The idea of rugged individualism encourages us to fake it. It encourages us to hide our weaknesses and failures. It teaches us to be utterly ashamed of our limitations. It drives us to attempt to be superwomen and supermen. ... It pushes us day in and day out to look as if 'we had it all together,' as if we were without needs and in total control of our lives. It relentlessly demands that we keep up appearances. It also relentlessly isolates us from each other."

~ *M. Scott Peck, The Different Drum: Community Making and Peace*

Mar 26, 2016 11:33am

Max on March 15 and today after two hours of dog-wrestling
Note the "I'll never trust you again" look on his face after his haircut

Apr 06, 2016 9:34am

The same day I found the lawn tractor I resurrected, I found a garden trailer someone had thrown away. Not much good in the condition I found it but potentially nice, with a tilting box for dumping. I could pull it behind my new lawn tractor.

The front wheels from the second lawn tractor, I used to replace the too-narrow wheels on the salvaged trailer, which would sink into soft turf. (The old wheels, I eventually mounted on the base of an anvil I built. They're perfect for that.)

For the new wheels, I needed an axle. Looking through my foraged steel, I found a one-inch diameter weight lifting bar I'd picked up a year or two ago.

The wheels take a 3/4-inch axle, so on my 10-inch Atlas machinist lathe (built in 1944, the first year they made them with a quick change gearbox), I turned the ends of the axle down to fit.

I disassembled the garden trailer and with an angle grinder, cut off unneeded parts to get down to what I wanted to use. I wire-wheeled the rust and old paint and brushed on fresh Rustoleum. Mounted the new axle and wheels and went to work on the new box, which will be 42 inches wide by 47 inches long by 12 inches deep, about double the original box.

To build the box, I'm using angle iron from old bed frames. The thing about bed frame angle iron is, it's hardened. Difficult to drill, even with cobalt steel drill bits. Easy enough to saw, though. The industrial blade on my horizontal band saw goes right through it.

About three fourths finished, my 5/16 inch cobalt steel drill bit was too dull to continue. I'm good at freehand sharpening on the grinder, but for this, I couldn't produce precise enough angles to hold up to the demand.

So I figured, time to get a drill bit sharpener. It turns out, the top-rated one is over a thousand dollars, and even a Drill Doctor, which some say is pretty bad, is over a hundred.

I looked at YouTube videos on shopmade drill bit sharpening jigs and figured out I could mount a grinding disk on a table saw and use the miter and blade angle settings to get the right geometry.

I remembered an old eight-inch Craftsman table saw I picked up at the transfer station a couple of years ago. That might work. Dragged it out and tried to figure out how the motor is supposed to mount. Online I found some pictures and a PDF of the user's manual, from the early 1950's.

OK. The motor that came with it is ancient. Probably runs, but it would be a project to renovate. And some of the mounting hardware is missing. From my collection, I dug out a Craftsman, half-horsepower motor with exactly the same mounting arrangement as my table saw. And all the correct mounting parts were there, including the ones missing from the other motor.

Reflecting, I remembered. One day when I was visiting the Amish farm down the road, Ananiah Hershberger showed me an old eight-inch Craftsman table saw he was converting to run with a lawn mower motor. He sold me the electric motor for five dollars. Exactly the motor this saw was missing. I plugged it in and it purred. No renovation needed.

Apr 9, 2016 11.31am

A month or so ago, I used the new lawn tractor to tow my old, beyond-repair lawn tractor to the transfer station. When I got there, Dan, who runs the place, said, "There's another lawn tractor just like your new one." And so there was. It wasn't in as good shape, didn't look restorable. "Would you mind if I strip off the parts I can use if I put what's left in the dumpster?" I asked. "Go ahead," he said.

I came back with my tools and spent a pleasant hour removing the seat, three wheels (the fourth was damaged) and the mowing deck deflector chute, which equipped me to upgrade my renovated lawn tractor to near pristine condition.

Checking the rear wheel I'd retrieved, I saw it has a like-new, 20-inch tire (Wal-Mart price: $66.80). The rear tires on the lawn tractor were 18 inches.

Driving it, the one thing I wasn't happy with was the top speed was a little too slow. Switching to 20-inch tires would increase the speed 11 percent, but where to get another wheel to go with the one I rescued from the dumpster?

After reconnoitering eBay and Craigslist, checking with Jim to see if he had any contacts, and eventually asking someone at the hardware store, I learned there's a large lawn equipment dealer about twenty minutes away.

Looking online, I saw it's a sophisticated, modern operation, not likely to have used parts for sale. But I called them anyway. The receptionist said, "Parts is busy right now. I'll put you through to service." I asked the service manager if there was any such thing as a lawn equipment salvage yard. He said, "There's one next store. He calls himself 'Ken's repairs.' I'll get you the number."

I called Ken, told him I was looking for a used rear wheel and tire to fit a Sears lawn tractor. "What size?" he asked. "Twenty by ten by eight," I said. "Yeah, I've got them." "How much?" I asked. "Twenty-five will do," he said.

I drove down and found the most wonderful junkyard. Farm tractors, lawn tractors, forklifts, etc. A fabulous assortment of machinery piled high, with narrow footpaths between. And a chicken coop.

Ken and I walked to the pile of lawn tractor wheels and tires just outside the front door. He walked over to one and said, "Here you go." It was perfect. I told him it was exactly like the one on my lawn tractor. "Probably came off a Sears just like yours," he said. "We get lots of them."

Apr 18, 2016 12:45pm

Over the weekend, I was a vendor at the New England Folk Festival. During a slow period, I got up from my table to stretch my legs. As I wandered the room, I noticed a brightly colored object on the floor, a little bigger than a quarter.

With my nearsightedness, I couldn't see it clearly, but it looked like there was writing on it. I leaned down to pick it up and saw it was a button, like a campaign button with a slogan that you pin to your shirt. It said ...

"If your life is so exciting, why are you reading this button?"

Apr 21, 2016 9:42pm

Today I finished building my precision drill bit sharpening setup made from a salvaged 1950's table saw and an electric motor I bought from Ananiah Hershberger.

At top right in the photo you can see the 5/16 inch drill bit I sharpened on the setup. The split point detail I ground with the Dremel wheel after doing the main sharpening on the table saw setup. The table saw miter gauge was set at 67-1/2 degrees to produce the appropriate 135 degree included angle of the drill point. The sawblade tilt was set to 14 degrees to produce the appropriate cutting-edge relief angle.

The grinding disc I made from 1/4 inch aluminum plate, which I turned round and then machined perfectly flat on my 1944 Atlas metalworking lathe. The abrasive is a self-stick silicon carbide 220 grit sanding disc.

I built the stand taller than you would want for sawing wood. It puts the worktable at a comfortable height to rest your forearms for steadiness and it positions you close to the work.

In the last photo, you can see the chassis is finished, with the wheels and tires I salvaged from a discarded lawn tractor. The wheels sit under the box, which is about twice as big as the original box.

Apr 23, 2016 8:04pm

On various projects, I was outside several hours today. In the woods across the road resides a very talkative cardinal.

Nonstop, hour after hour, he proclaimed, "Whatwhatwhatwhat CHEER! CHEER! CHEER! Whatwhatwhatwhatwhatwhatwhatwhat ... Whatwhatwhat-what CHEER! CHEER! CHEER! Whatwhatwhatwhatwhatwhatwhatwhat ..." relentlessly, on and on.

For the first hour or so, I enjoyed his exuberance without thinking much about it. Then I began to wonder, "What's he saying?" Now and then between his calls you could hear other cardinals in the distance calling back.

He was saying, "Here I am! I'm here. Is anybody over there? I'm still here. Here I am! Can anybody hear me? I hear you! Here I am! Are you still there? Here I am!"

This went on and on. I wondered, "Doesn't this cardinal have anything else to do?" Then it dawned on me. Rather sad, when you think about it. I've seen this behavior before. The poor bird is addicted to social media.

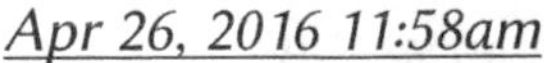

Apr 26, 2016 11:58am

Made almost entirely from found and salvaged materials including the lawn tractor (discarded because of a blown head gasket), trailer chassis (discarded because the box had rusted out), trailer box frame (discarded bed frame angle iron), wheels/tires (salvaged from another scrapped lawn tractor), trailer axle (salvaged weightlifting bar), paint ("oops" paint sold at a fraction because of a tinting error), etc.

Apr 27, 2016 10:44am

My new sewing machine. Seventeen dollars at the Salvation Army Store. MUCH better than my old one. It only needed the tensions adjusted and it works perfectly. Powerful, runs fast and smooth, doesn't bog down, even through belt loops on blue jeans.

Apr 27, 2016 2:12pm

Here comes the sun ...

Apr 28, 2016 8:45am

"Max," I said, "you're famous."

"Then can I have your breakfast?" he asked.

Apr 28, 2016 3:51pm

From his repose, Max jumped up excitedly when the school bus stopped at our drive. He ran downstairs to greet the girls, but only Mahlet got off.

Max came back to my room, plopped down on his chair and resumed moping. I explained that today is Thursday and Natasha and Maria come on the late bus on Thursday. Max asked, "Is Thursday something to eat?" "Sorry, Max, no," I said. "You can't eat a day of the week."

Mahlet came in and fussed over him awhile and then left. Max resumed moping. A little later, I asked him, "Can I get you anything?" "More children, please," he said.

May 04, 2016 5:41pm

I returned from errands to find Isabella lingering in front of Maria's bedroom door. I knocked and heard Maria say, "What?" I also heard a thump, which is the familiar sound of Max jumping down off Maria's bed.

I opened the door. Isabella went in and Max came out.

I went to talk to Arleen for a minute. Then, as I walked toward my office, Max followed me. "Want to hang out?" I asked him. Apparently not. Max stopped following me and lingered in front of Maria's door. I knocked. "What?" I heard Maria say.

I opened the door. Max went in and Isabella came out.

Which is to say, despite the appearance of much activity, nothing whatsoever happened.

May 06, 2016 6:38pm

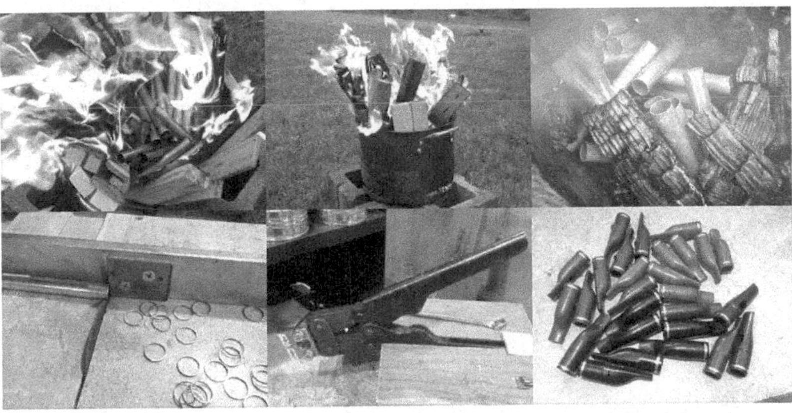

People often ask, "What do you do when you tweak a whistle?"*

One of the things I do is press a brass ring around the whistlehead socket so it won't crack. No one's ever asked, "How do you make the brass rings?"

I have to enlarge available brass tubing to the right size, but first I have to make the metal soft enough to work. For that, I made an annealing oven from a kitchen stew pot. To get the fire to burn, I cut slots near the bottom so air would come in from underneath and draw up through the fire in an updraft chimney effect.

After annealing, I swage the tubing with dies that mount in my milling machine, using the mill's quill to press the die through the tube. The dies are made from steel bar, turned on my lathe to the right shape and diameter.

Then I slice the rings, about .065 inches wide, on a little table saw I built to cut tubing.

I deburr inside the rings with a Dremel tool and then press the rings around the whistlehead sockets using a plumbing compression ring tool I modified for the purpose, with interchangeable jaws I machined to fit each size ring.

For the final bright brass finish, I spin the whistleheads on the lathe and touch the rings with a fine file.

So there you have it. (I'm glad we cleared that up.)

*See appendix for more about how I tweak a whistle.

May 09, 2016 2:26pm

This morning as the girls were getting ready for school, I heard Arleen say, "Here's scrambled eggs for you."

Eventually, the sounds of scurrying children settled down and I heard the diesel of the bus. Soon after, Max showed up, as he does every morning when the children leave the house, carrying his plush bear. He had the wild look in his eye that means I'm required to play tug-of-war/throw-the-bear.

A little later, as I was working at my desk, I heard whimpering.

"What's wrong, Max?" I asked him. He came over and gave a pleading look. Then he turned and took a few steps, looking back to see if I would follow him.

"OK, Max. Show me." I said.

Max led me to Maria's door and squirmed impatiently.

"Maria's gone to school," I said. I opened the door so he could see the room was empty.

Max rushed in and ran in circles. I knew instantly, this was not about Maria.

In two seconds, he zeroed in on Maria's dresser and stood on his hind legs. And there it was. Maria's half eaten plate of scrambled eggs.

<u>May 14, 2016 6:17pm</u>

Flow ...

Two summers ago I began the reconquest of parts of our property that had succumbed to invasive Japanese knotweed. There were three areas, two smallish and the third extensive, under an impenetrable jungle of eight-foot-tall knotweed.

Each summer, I've dug out more of the rhizomes until now there are still many small shoots, but none with the vigor and size of the original growth. I can control them with a lawnmower. The first summer, the largest rhizome I unearthed weighed twenty-eight pounds. The remaining ones I find nowadays are just small roots.

I had read that young knotweed shoots are edible, so this spring I harvested some. They looked and cooked like pink asparagus and were delicious. But despite the pleasantness of eating, both Arleen and I found there was something about them that didn't agree.

So there would be no point maintaining a controlled crop of knotweed. The young shoots indicated where the remaining roots were, so I figured, now's the time to dig them out. As I worked my way across one of the smaller patches, perhaps thirty feet across, I observed there was hardly any vegetation. When the knotweed was tall, it had shaded everything out.

I wondered, rather than seeding grass, what might I plant there we could eat? It's a lot of work to break sod for gardening. It would be a wasted opportunity not to plant something.

Last fall, I harvested perhaps 100,000 lamb's quarters seeds. It took about ten minutes, which gives an idea how prodigious a seed producer they are. Lamb's quarters is a wild relative of spinach, much easier to grow, and I like it better. It grows by itself wherever there is broken ground, which means it should be nearly effortless to cultivate.

I watched the patch through a day's cycle and saw, though it's close to the trees along the creek, it gets almost uninterrupted sunlight. Perfect for lamb's quarters. But before I could sow the seeds, I would have to burn off the brush pile I had accumulated next to the patch. So I called the town and got a burn permit.

Today, I ran a garden hose down to the area, mowed around the brush pile, soaked the surrounding ground and set the pile alight. In addition to the brush, much of the pile was knotweed roots, which I wanted to consume completely so they wouldn't start new colonies.

In the main garden was a pile of dried vegetation I wanted to burn. As I gathered the garden pile, I came across a large black-eyed Susan I had intended to transplant. Now would be the time, since I'll be tilling there soon. After putting the vegetation on the fire, I got the shovel and moved the black-eyed Susan to the bed along the driveway.

I keep two buckets there because Arleen has planted herbs nearby and needs the water to tend them. Watering the black-eyed Susans emptied the buckets so I brought them down to the hose, filled them and carried them back.

Returning to my fire, I saw the brush was almost consumed but the knotweed roots were hardly affected. What to do? The rule is you're only allowed to burn brush under three inches diameter and other vegetation generally, but not wood waste. Well, Japanese knotweed is a listed, noxious, invasive species. Seems to me, it would be appropriate to use any reasonable means to eradicate it.

So I went to my woodshop and hauled out two bins full of wood scraps. They made a nice, roaring fire but still didn't consume all the knotweed roots. So I went back to the shop, sorted through a pile of small pieces and put another load on the fire.

That seemed to do the trick. After another round of blazing, the fire settled down to a small pile of glowing embers and ash. Success. And my wood shop is tidy now.

In between tending the fire and the various other side projects of the day, I did sow some lamb's quarters seeds. The literature I've read says they typically sprout in two or three days.

Oh, and I discovered, mice have made a bowling alley in our hay field.

May 14, 2016 8:31pm

Look what I found in the hayfield. And by the look of it, I'm not the first to find it. Note the tiny tooth marks around the finger holes!

May 15, 2016 6:34pm

There were seventeen turkeys in our yard a month or so ago. Then they all disappeared. They're sitting on eggs now, for another week or two. When they're hatched, we'll see how many come back to visit us again.

Turkeys are into community parenting, so you get a flock of however many hens, three or six or a dozen, along with a ridiculously large number of cute, fuzzy poults clamoring around them.

They have a regular route. In the morning they come down the hill across the road into our yard, work their way along our driveway, sometimes hanging out on the pavement awhile before continuing down the slope. Gradually they proceed back to the woods by the stream. Then toward evening, they work the same route in reverse, eventually heading back into the woods across the street to roost for the night.

Often they browse the whole area close by, circumnavigating the house. Early spring, there are a lot of wood ticks, but after the turkeys have fed for a few weeks, we see very few.

May 16, 2016 10:03am

I fed the crows this morning as usual.

Then I went over to the area where I'd dug out knotweed, sowed lamb's quarters and burned brush.

I've been thinking. Arleen's started more "patio" zucchini than will fit in the planter boxes around the deck. I don't want to put them in the main garden because they're a variety that stays small and won't climb the trellis I've placed for squash and cukes.

So I'm thinking I'll plant them down there near the lamb's quarters.

After I put out breakfast for the crows, I turned over the ground where the brush had burned. I've a broadfork I bought last season that works well for that. Spares the earthworms (motorized tillers kill them) and goes pretty fast. Makes a nice bed for planting.

As I worked, I could hear the crows nearby in the trees conversing. Discussing how inconvenient it is that the human leaves food but then hangs around and makes us wait before we can have some privacy to eat. Most inconsiderate!

Later, as I sat here at my desk, I saw a single crow walk casually up the driveway. I wondered, "Why is he walking? He can fly!" He meandered up the driveway, then strolled off the side into the grass, turned again and walked back toward the house through the lawn. That's exactly where I'd mowed yesterday evening. He was looking around to see what I'd done there. Inspecting my work.

May 16, 2016 12:42pm

Yesterday evening I lay down to rest awhile. Max came in and searched around the room. "Mahlet," I called. "Would you please toss Max's pillow in here? He's left it in the hallway." Mahlet came in with the pillow, fussed over Max and left again.

The pillow came from the family room downstairs. When it became Max's personal pillow and how it got upstairs, nobody knows.

<u>*May 18, 2016 7:56pm*</u>

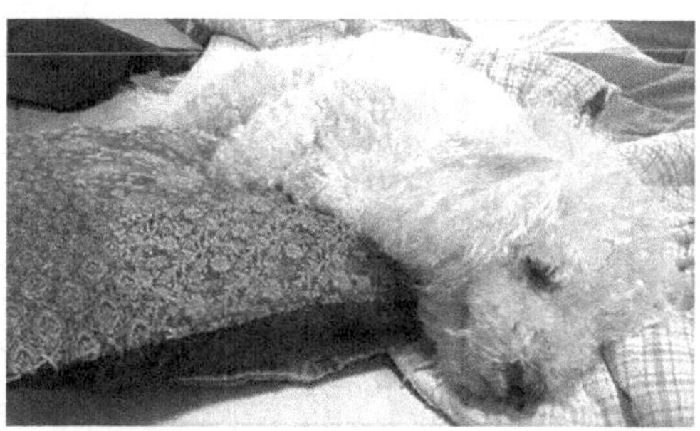

A dog and his pillow at the end of a busy day

<u>*May 25, 2016 8:23am*</u>

A wild turkey hen with ten new poults just meandered up my driveway. She's the first I've seen this season after the hens all disappeared to sit on their eggs.

<u>*May 28, 2016 9:06am*</u>

Day before yesterday I mowed a path between the enclosed garden and the squash patch next to the woods by the stream. I made the path is so I can run hose for a soaker watering system.

As I mowed the knee-deep hay, I worried I might disturb some creature's nest, but thankfully I got through OK.

This morning after I visited the squash patch, as I walked back toward the garden enclosure, I heard squawking and saw motion nearby. There was the turkey hen who had appeared a few days ago with her ten poults. Around her the poults skittered as they moved slowly away from me.

Then, as I continued toward the house, from across the garden I saw frantic fluttering in the corner of the enclosure. A poult had gotten tangled in the deer netting!

As I approached, I saw the poult wasn't entangled, but had somehow gotten inside the garden and couldn't find a way out. I easily caught the little creature, which settled in my hands as I cradled it.

I carried the excited little ball of downy feathers to the edge of the hay where its mother waited, calling out. I put the poult down on the path. As it scrambled into the hay toward its mother, I could hear their conversation, the mother hen calling out in little squawks and the poult exclaiming, "Peep, Peep, Peep! Peep, Peep, Peep!"

May 28, 2016 8:28pm

You may recall, a few weeks ago, I sowed a bed of lamb's quarters seed in the area I'd cleared of Japanese knotweed.

Lamb's quarters, aka "wild spinach," is one of the easiest of all vegetables to grow, as my recent experience demonstrates:

Every day since sowing, I've checked where I sowed the seed, but no lamb's quarters have emerged. There are a few grass seedlings beginning to grow there, but no lamb's quarters, despite the fact that I sowed hundreds of seeds.

However, the squash mounds, where I DIDN'T sow seed, have erupted with lamb's quarters!

Which PROVES lamb's quarters is the easiest of all vegetables to grow. The secret to an abundant crop of lamb's quarters is, don't do anything at all!

May 29, 2016 11:20am

Avian Flight Plan Logistics and Lawn Tractor Placement: an observational hypothesis ...

I had to move the lawn tractor. I'd been parking it near the wild rose thicket, in which an as yet undetermined number of birds are nesting.

There was a heavy rain yesterday, which washed away some of the evidence, but the photo is still indicative. Before the rain, an impressive amount of poop had piled up on the dashboard. Based on this evidence, I conclude that the birds' flight plan was:

1. Emerge from wild rose thicket.
2. Perch on lawn tractor steering wheel.
3. Poop.
4. Take off toward destination.

Clearly, the evidence indicates this was a systematic, repetitive behavior. But why?

Well it's a lot of work, flying. By sheer muscle power, you have to get your entire body weight airborne. You wouldn't want to bring along anything you don't need, now would you?

But you wouldn't want to leave it back at the nest, either. Wouldn't be a very nice place to raise the kids if you did that! Ideally, you want a nice perch just ten or so feet away from the nest so you can make a quick stopover, dump your excess baggage and then be on your way.

May 31, 2016 7:19am

Two flamingos were flying over a kingdom. One said to the other, "Of what sort is this Raikva, the cart bearer?"

The other answered, "Just as in a game of dice, all the lower casts of the dice go over to the one who has won the krita-cast, whatever meritorious act is performed by anyone in this kingdom, the merit from the act accrues to the doer of the act, and it also accrues to Raikva, because he is a knower of Brahman."

The king overheard this and sent his ministers out to find Raikva. They came back and told the king, "He is nowhere to be found." The king sent them out again, saying, "Search for him where knowers of Brahman are to be found."

They went out again and found Raikva, the knower of Brahman, lying in the shade under his cart, scratching an itch.

~ *Chandogya Upanishad*

Jun 01, 2016 6:01pm

Heading home after a busy day browsing the hayfield ...

Jun 02, 2016 3:16pm

I love crows.

In 1986, when I was with Maharishi Mahesh Yogi in India, a few of us were sitting outside the dining enclosure sipping juice and trying to stay cool in 107 degrees. That was all you could do in the middle of the day.

There was a water buffalo tied to a tree nearby and a gang of crows in the tree were entertaining themselves with The Water Buffalo Game.

It goes like this ...

Ten or so birds were arrayed up and down the branches of the tree. The bottommost bird would drop onto the water buffalo's back and work his way up the buffalo's neck to the buffalo's head.

The idea was to get as far as you could before the buffalo shook his head. The birds took turns at this, each working its way down the tree from the top to bottom as the last bird to play went back to the end of the line at the top of the tree.

The best players could get all the way to the buffalo's nose before he shook his head.

We watched this for about half an hour.

The next day, the water buffalo was gone and the birds had moved onto the next game. It had rained during the night. A hundred feet or so from where they played the buffalo game was a wheelbarrow full of water from the rain.

I couldn't see exactly what the crows were doing, but they made a noisy fuss entertaining themselves with the water in the wheelbarrow.

Jun 02, 2016 11:10pm

Yesterday evening I drove Natasha and Maria and their friend Brianna to drop them off at school for a chorus concert.

On the way, a bushy-tailed animal darted across the road in front of us.

"What was THAT?" I exclaimed.

"Squirrel?" Maria asked.

"That was no squirrel," I said, backing the car near to where the animal had run into the shrubbery. "Is it still there?" I asked.

"It's a fox!" Natasha exclaimed.

Looking through the back window, I saw it was indeed a brownish gray fox, in no hurry at all, sniffing calmly around the area right next to us by the road, looking at us occasionally and then going back to her business.

When the fox had disappeared, we continued to the high school. Approaching, we saw activity on one of the sports fields. Natasha said, "There are tryouts for something. What do you try out for this time of year?" Maria said, "They're little kid tryouts. They have them around now."

I said, "I would like to try out to be a little kid. Why wasn't I notified about this? I would make a great little kid."

"Yeah, totally," Maria said. "You would blend right in."

Jun 03, 2016 8:56am

(From three years ago)

Jumping spider ...

Yesterday in the heat, I helped the children retrieve their wading pool from under the deck.

Along the way, I noticed a towel that had blown down onto the grass, having been hung to dry on the deck railing. I put the towel around my neck like a scarf and continued with the pool.

Ana, alarmed, said, "There's a big spider right by your neck!"

Looking down, I saw a fine specimen of a jumping spider, almost as big as my thumb, perched there on the towel.

I love jumping spiders.

This affair began many years ago.

When camping, I was sitting in the shade and noticed a tiny jumping spider had drifted onto my hand. I positioned my hand fingertips up, knowing that many such creatures like to climb to the top off things.

And so he did. The tiny jumping spider proceeded straightaway to my fingertip. I watched him there, and suddenly, he was on a different fingertip. I didn't see how he got there. He was just on one fingertip and then somehow, he rematerialized on another fingertip, instantaneously.

I spread my fingertips, and discovered he could jump remarkably far, relative to his tiny body size. Back and forth, so quickly I never saw him jump.

I wondered whether one could play this game with big jumping spiders, but I was afraid to try until I heard a radio interview with an arachnologist who explained that, with a few dangerous exceptions, most spiders don't bite. Among others, he talked about jumping spiders.

A component of their prodigious jumping ability is the fact that they see very well, and they see further than most other spiders.

I put my hand up to the spider, inviting him to step onto it.

He touched my hand tentatively with one "foot" and then, sensing body heat, drew it back quickly.

Then he did something that amazed me.

He whirled around and looked directly into my face.

He held eye contact for several seconds. Then he turned back around and again placed a tentative foot on my hand. Again sensing body heat, he again whirled around and looked into my face, held eye contact again for several seconds, then turned back around and again cautiously checked my hand.

He did this several times, and then eventually, after holding eye contact one more time, he turned around again and stepped onto my hand. I carried him to the tall grass, during which excursion he sat calmly on my palm without trying to get away. I put my hand down, and he jumped off into the grass.

Jun 03, 2016 10:16am

For a few days, due to an accounting mishap, I can't use my checking account to pay bills. But the bills have to be paid nonetheless.

I called Capital One MasterCard to ask about other ways to make my upcoming payment.

A telephone robot asked, "In a few words, please say what you are calling about."

"Payment method," I said.

"You want to ask about making a payment, is that correct?"

"Yes," I said.

"I'm sorry, I didn't get that. Do you want to ask about making a payment?"

"Yeess," I said, slowly and clearly, speaking directly into the phone.

"I'm sorry, I didn't get that. Do you want to ask about making a payment?"

"Yes," I said again.

"I'm sorry, I didn't get that. Do you want to ask about making a payment?"

"YESSSS!!!!!!" I screamed at the top of my lungs.

"Got it," the robot said, in a calm, matter-of-fact voice.

Jun 05, 2016 7:39pm

My accidental fern garden

When we moved onto the property, there was an overgrown dirt pile left from the construction three years earlier. On the north side of the dirt pile grew a colony of ferns.

Two summers ago I borrowed my neighbor's tractor and moved the dirt pile to the garden plot, to level the southeast corner. I took care not to disturb the ferns, which I can see from my office window. They give me much pleasure.

This spring I noticed there were almost no fiddleheads emerging, and I thought the ferns might have died away because the sunlight is different than when the dirt pile shaded them.

But I thought, "If they're still there, I can help them by scalping the competing grass and weeds before the fiddleheads have begun to come up."

Shortly after, they did come up, and they're thriving without the competition. I'm hopeful they'll eventually shade out the turf underneath and dominate the area without my having to tend them.

The only other plant that seems to have benefited from my mowing down the grass there is milkweed, which has come up amid the ferns in some numbers.

Wouldn't it be wonderful if I could transform that accidental growth into a permanent fern/milkweed garden that will attract monarch butterflies?

Jun 07, 2016 10:10pm

I picked up a hooker today ...

I'm making an assumption but from all appearances and the questions she asked, I think she's probably turning tricks to survive.

You hardly ever see a woman hitchhiking.

I'd seen this woman on the same spot a week or so ago, maybe in her forties, looking battleworn. I'd been driving the opposite way; when I came back from my errand, she was gone.

Today I pulled over, removed some items from the passenger seat, and she got in. She asked if I was going up Route 32. "Yes," I said. "Where are you going?"

"Eagleville. I just need to get something to eat and drink."

"I can take you to Eagleville," I said.

As we drove along, she asked, "Where are you from?"

I named my town.

"Where are you going?" she asked.

"I was going home, but I'm happy to take you to Eagleville," I said.

"Do you live alone?" she asked.

"No, I've got a family," I said.

"How many?" she asked.

"There are five of us," I said.

"It's nice to have family," she said.

I thought of the times I'd been alone and how I'd suffered. I thought of what a blessing it is to be among people you deeply care about.

"I'd be terribly lonely without my family," I said.

I thought, "What a tactless thing to say to a homeless woman. Well, I can't take the words back, can I? I hope I didn't hurt her."

"I've got family, too," she said. "Just, there are some things ..."

I tried to make small talk, but there was no connection. An exchange of comments, but not really a conversation. She asked if there's a mirror in the sunshade. I flipped it down to show her. She checked her makeup and hair and asked, "Is it supposed to rain?"

I'd checked earlier to see if I would need to water the plantings, so I was able to recite the next several hours' prediction.

"Where do you want me to drop you off?" I asked as we neared Eagleville.

"Eagleville Pizza," she said. "I think that's what it's called."

"College Pizza," I corrected her. It's not far from the University of Connecticut. "I'll give you some money so you can get a good meal."

"Thank you. God bless you," she said. Her words were distant, flat, an empty recitation of a memorized line. She seemed spent, gone, emotionally shut off, as though a freight load of troubles had buried her feeling heart.

We drove past where I remembered the pizza place to be.

"There are some places further up ahead," she said.

"The next town is pretty far," I said. "Where do you want me to drop you?"

"There's a bar and a pizza place and a Dunkin' Donuts."

I didn't like the idea of dropping her off at a bar.

We continued driving. She pulled a flip-phone cellphone from her purse and fiddled with it. I was surprised to see the phone.

"Mom, it's me," she said. "Dad tried to call earlier. What's wrong?"

She said a few more sentences and put the phone back in her purse. It took awhile for me to figure out, the cellphone is a prop. There was no phone call, no mom, no dad. Just a dead flip-phone she'd picked up somewhere.

We approached Willington.

"It's on the left," she said "The pizza place where all the college kids go."

I saw a little row of shops, and a fairly upscale looking pizza parlor. It had a carved and painted wooden sign with gilded letters: "Willington Pizza."

I pulled into the parking lot and pulled out the only cash in my pocket, a twenty dollar bill. One of my errands had been to pick up a twenty for Arleen to cover half of a restaurant tab from yesterday. One of the grown children had visited and Arleen had gone somewhere to lunch with her, Natasha and Maria.

"God bless you," she said flatly.

Later I figured out, she'd lied about wanting to go to Eagleville. If she'd told me she wanted to go to Willington, it would have been too far to ask, so she finessed the ride by asking me to take her to Eagleville and then stringing me along the rest of the way.

As I drove home, I thought about two things:

1. Where could I stop, buy a small item of food and get twenty dollars cash back on my debit card? It wouldn't do to go home and tell Arleen I'd given her twenty dollars to a prostitute.

2. Had I done anything for that woman, or had I only rubbed salt in an open wound?

Finally I concluded, I did what I could.

If my thoughtless words, instead of consoling, had made her feel more isolated and lonely, perhaps that was what she needs to feel. If she is ever to escape her situation, some feeling inside will have to motivate her.

But I would never presume to try something like that on purpose. In any case, she's likely developed a thick skin. I'm inclined to think the net result of my gesture is, she got a ride and twenty dollars.

Here's a prayer for a forlorn woman, far away from home:

Teardrops fell on momma's note
When I read the things she wrote
She said "we miss you hon', we love you
Come on home"

All these years and all these roads
Never led me back to you
I'm always five hundred miles away from home
Away from home, away from home
Always out here on my own
I'm still five hundred miles away from home

Jun 08, 2016 11:01am

(From three years ago)

Yesterday Maria told me there was going to be a party at Brianna's house today.

I told her, "I've too much work to be able to drive, but if Brianna's mom (Tina) is willing to come get you, you can go."

This morning, Maria told me the party's at two, Natasha's also invited and Tina will pick them up.

I told the girls the house needs to be tidy before there can be any parties, and I need to talk to Tina. When I called, Tina told me the arrangement was news to her, and she wouldn't be able to drive the girls because she was going to be busy running the party. I said, "That's what I figured. So the girls made up the part about you picking them up." I told Natasha and Maria there wasn't a ride, so they wouldn't be able to go. I expected them to be grumpy about it, especially since they'd already cleaned the house, but they seemed OK.

Then Ana came in and said, "Can we paint my room today?" I thought about it and said, "Well I promised, so let's do it now." I asked which walls she wanted to paint and she said, just the one wall, with the two windows. I put her to work getting things ready and I sanded and spackled the pinholes. As I was painting, I commented to Ana, "You seemed to know right where that lavender paint was. You brought it here in seconds." She said, "Yeah. I've been watching that bucket of paint for two years."

The project took about two and a half hours. Most of the time, Natasha and Maria sat on Ana's bed and watched me. Enthusiastically. As I was painting, I thought, "They're having as much fun watching me paint this wall as they would have had at the party."

After I finished painting, I heard Ana pestering Mahlet to go outside with her. "The doctor told me I watch too much video and I need to get more exercise, so come outside with me." I was there at Ana's school physical. What the doctor actually said was, "Be sure to get plenty of exercise and don't watch too much TV." Ana said, "I wonder how she could tell I wasn't getting enough exercise."

As I was working at my desk, through the open window I heard Ana exclaim, "They're so CUTE!" Later, I found Ana and Mahlet sitting on the front porch, watching five cottontail rabbits only a few feet away. There were two adults and three babies, eating a carrot the girls had given them.

Jun 14, 2016 8:17am

(After the shootings in Orlando)

I hardly know what to say in the face of such terrible news. Here are a couple of things ...

There are two levels of response, and in my opinion, both are important.

On one level, our greatest responsibility is to rise to a level of awakened inner clarity that, whatever we do, our natural influence radiates harmony and coherence and helps elevate collective consciousness everywhere, whether we are moving in the world or secluded in retreat.

How to do that, I'll not try to say. Ultimately, it is something each of us must sort out for ourselves. In my opinion, it is the most important thing in this life. On the level of Being, of silent, eternal pure consciousness, we are all interconnected, and from that level we have the greatest influence.

But regardless of whether a person's vocation is monastic or worldly, it is important not to conflate harmony with separation. A spirituality that shuts out the world of human turmoil is not yet fully mature, not yet fully empowered either for one's own enlightenment or for the good of humanity.

(The great monastics did not, do not, leave the world to escape it. They with-drew into contemplation and prayer to heal not only themselves, but the en-tire world as well.)

On the other level, each of us is compelled to act in one way or another. How we act, what we do and say, will naturally reflect our own inner state, whether turbulent or serene, confused or clear.

So first is the project of getting ourselves to clarity. There is no end point; noth-ing ever becomes "perfectly clear." But events like these (along with a great many others) should impel us to think, to try to understand, and especially, to FEEL.

When we are able to awaken to our own connectedness with, interdepend-ence with, every other soul, then we are in the best position to do the greatest good. Because when we are awake to that connection, then we concretely feel, we know, we directly see, we ARE every other soul, there is no "other," and we are the world.

"Whatsoever you do to the least of these, that you do unto Me."

In the force of such an awareness, how can we not act?

Jun 16, 2016 11:51am

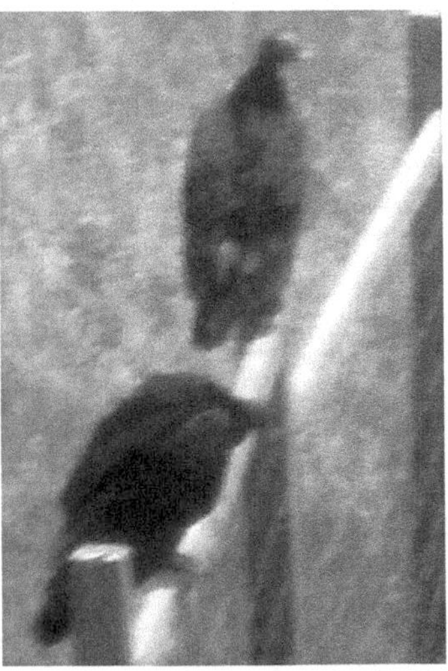

A pair of cute little turkey vultures admiring my vegetable garden just now

Vultures, I must confess, are my favorite birds. I've watched them closely. They have a goofy, apologetic manner, as if to say, "Oh, dear. There you are, LOOKING at me. This is so embarrassing. I'm sorry. I know it's unseemly, but somebody's got to clean up this mess. OK, you're still there. I'll just go over here a little ways off and you can do whatever you need to do. Don't mind me. I'm just a poor little turkey vulture. Take your time. No bother. I'll just come back whenever you're finished."

I've wondered, why do vultures act that way?

Well, consider this. Vultures often feed from other predators' kills. In fact, vultures don't hunt, and they don't kill. They're not really predators at all. They're scavengers. It would be important that the real predator, the actual owner of the kill, not feel threatened. It seems to me, vultures accomplish this by signaling in as many ways as possible, "I'm insignificant. Nothing to worry about. Really. Don't mind me at all."

Jun 16, 2016 10:23pm

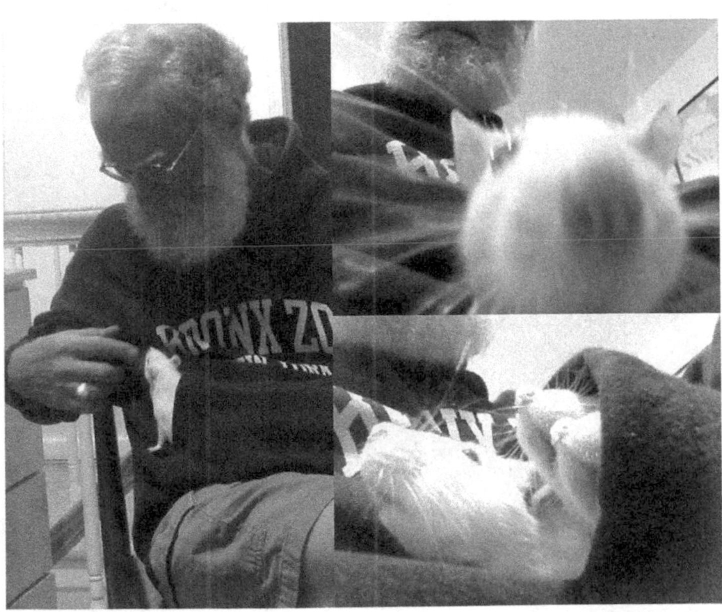

Hangin' out

Jun 17, 2016 9:06am

"Max," I said, "are you comfortable?"
"Maria's taking too much of the bed. Could you ask her to please stop crowding me?"

Jun 17, 2016 9:53am

Again this morning, when I go to weed the squash patch, I see the wild turkey hen and her ten or so poults that have been browsing our hayfield. The poults scramble into the tall grass, but the hen just calmly walks a little distance and then stands, keeping eye contact. I speak softly to her, and she appears to listen.

Jun 18, 2016 5:16pm

"Would you PLEASE talk to Maria? She's crowding me again!"

Jun 18, 2016 7:54pm

(From three years ago)

The children and I have pet rats.

Some months ago, I purchased a young female rat to accompany another rat who'd lost her cage mate. (Rats are social animals and aren't happy alone.) I'd recently watched "To Kill a Mockingbird" and suggested we name her Boo.

Boo, as it turned out, was pregnant.

She gave birth to Loretta, Daryl Short, Daryl Long (identical except for the length of the white tip of their tails), Ziggy, Blob (identical except for the shape of the white patch on their bellies, which are, respectively, a zigzag and a blob) and Scruffy. These are the world's friendliest rats, since we started playing with them when they were babies.

Boo's daughters Daryl Short and Daryl Long entertain a visitor

Boo never grew much. Her babies are now much bigger than she is. I think she gave birth too young and sacrificed too much of her energy for those babies.

And she has respiratory trouble, which has needed a lot of care. I've saved her life a few times, worked out a system for nebulizer treatments, researched medication protocols, designed an air filtration system for her cage.

Boo is a little, nondescript, brown rat. In the wild, only one in twenty rats lives out its potential lifespan, due to predation, illness and mishaps. So in the grand scheme of the Universe, Boo isn't very important.

But she's MY little, nondescript, brown rat, and she's important to me.

I mix her medicine with rice or almond non-dairy ice cream and offer it to her on a spoon. Sometimes she'll take it and sometimes she won't. Sometimes she will only take it off my fingertip, standing on her little hind paws and holding my finger with her little forepaws while she licks the mixture off my fingertip.

Caring for this fragile little creature calls up an especially quiet and tender state of mind, which I find profoundly therapeutic and nourishing. I don't suppose this little rat cares all that much about me. She's used to me, comfortable with me, puts up with me, but other rats I've owned were more sociable.

I was thinking yesterday as I was taking care of her, what a privilege it is that this little creature allows me to spend this time with her every day.

Jun 18, 2016 9:55am

From the wild rose thicket below my window, comes an incessant "Meow! Meow! Meow! Meow! Meow! Meow! Meow! ... ."

One of my favorite birds ...

A few days ago, as I worked in the driveway, I saw her sitting on the tailgate of my utility trailer, watching me. I approached and talked softly to her. She stayed and allowed me to come near. I wondered if she didn't fly away because she has a nest she wants to say close to, in the rose thicket the trailer's parked beside.

Then a few days later, I was mowing near the rose thicket and saw her again, this time flitting excitedly about nearby. "Yeah," I thought. "For sure she's got a nest in there."

Jun 27, 2016 11:14am

Somehow, years ago, I discovered a message embedded in "The Star Spangled Banner." This turned into a little device the Universe uses to pass a signal when the fog of war occasionally overshadows my world.

Setting aside the patriotic meaning, what could "And the rockets' red glare, the bombs bursting in air, gave proof through the night that our flag was still there ... ." refer to?

"The Star Spangled Banner" comes up in my soundscape often enough, odds are I'll hear it when I'm in distress. Regardless of probability and coincidence, the seeming synchronicity comes across as a message from God, speaking directly to me.

The effect is instantaneous and always snaps me back to the assurance that "all is well and wisely put."

For me, the flag in the song is a metaphor, and the message is, God's perfect love, signified by the ever waving flag, is ever abiding, ALWAYS, in all circumstances, even when, for a moment, we can't see it.

Jun 28, 2016 1:59pm

Couple weeks ago, on one of my pilgrimages to the recycling transfer station around the corner, I noticed some Victorian looking decorative iron castings. On closer inspection, they turned out to be a pair of garden bench ends.

It would be a simple matter to bolt in new wooden slats and reassemble them into a functional bench. Alongside the construction materials dumpster, I saw someone had left some five quarters by six deck boards long enough for the project. A free garden bench kit! All materials included.

Here's the bench. Mother turkey was kind enough to pose in the foreground. Then she and her poults paraded around awhile so I could take more pictures. Following them, I came upon one of our wild blackberry thickets, which I was pleased to discover is now producing ripe berries.

Garden and hayfield seen from bench

Jun 29, 2016 7:59pm

Since I've pointed it out, Arleen is becoming familiar with the catbird who lives in the wild rose thicket by the driveway. The other day, she said, "I was working down in the garden and saw another catbird."

"I don't think that's a different bird," I said. "I think she followed you."

This evening I worked awhile in the garden enclosure. After I finished the task I'd started, I thought, "I should do some mowing." As I approached the lawn-mower, just a short distance from where I'd been working, I saw my catbird fly up from the mower's handlebar where she'd been sitting. I hadn't noticed her there as I worked, but she was watching me.

Truth be told, these last few days I'd been getting tired of listening to the incessant meowing under my window. "Catbirds aren't as interesting as crows," I thought. "All she does is sit in the thicket and meow all day long."

But this is a game changer. A wild bird that follows me around! How cool is that?

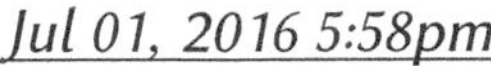

Jul 01, 2016 5:58pm

Overlooking the deck, juvenile barn swallows line up for supper. They wait while their parents swoop and circle over the hayfield gathering bugs. Then as Mom and Dad swing back to bring the next mouthful, they twitter and flap wildly, "Me! Me! MEEEE!"

Jul 02, 2016 7:16am

7:00 am view from the deck
Mother Turkey preens in the morning sun
The barn swallow kids line up for breakfast

Jul 03, 2016 8:38am

Downy hummingwoodpeckerbird

(8:30 am view from window over deck)

Jul 05, 2016 4:39pm

"I salute the light within your eyes where the whole universe dwells. For when you are at that center within you and I am at that place within me, we shall be one."

~ *Chief Crazy Horse, Oglala Sioux, 1877*

Namaste: "The divine in me salutes the divine in you."

~ *traditional Hindu greeting*

Jul 05, 2016 5:41pm

The five barn swallow kids have passed their driving tests and graduated.

This morning they were conspicuously absent from the breakfast lineup on the rain gutter over the deck. This evening, as I sit here watching, seven barn swallows circle and dive over the driveway outside my window, doing their part to manage the mosquito population.

Jul 06, 2016 10:03am

The barn swallow kids discussing today's flight plan ...

Jul 08, 2016 6:22pm

First time this season I've seen mother turkeys teaming up on daycare. In past years I've often seen several hens together with their young.

I know both these broods. (There are two, distinct sizes of poults. In the picture, it's hard to see the smaller ones.) One of the bigger poults, I held in my hands when she was very small, rescued her from the garden's deer netting. I haven't seen the older poults in a few weeks, the younger brood in a week or so. I wonder where they've been.

Jul 08, 2016 7:20pm

We are overrun with zucchini. The situation is dire, but we are soldiering on.

Jul 09, 2016 1:26pm

Catbird seat

Jul 10, 2016 5:07pm

Just now

The second hen is in the foliage on the left. Including her, I count thirteen turkeys. I think there are a few more poults in the foliage as well.

Jul 11, 2016 6:07pm

Jim mowed the hayfield today, much to the delight of the barn swallows and this fox who feast on the bugs and mice.

Jul 13, 2016 7:17am

6:35 am. I look out my window to see the wild turkeys casually working their way down the slope toward the hayfield, pausing to browse the blackberry thicket. I'm pleased to see them. The hayfield was mowed day before yesterday. I was hoping the interruption wouldn't disturb their routine.

They seem to follow a regular formation. The poults fan out ahead, one hen follows close behind the poults, and the other hen lags back and catches up later. Today she took extra long feasting on blackberries. She seemed oblivious to the others getting further and further away, but then she finished and caught up again. The invisible bond of motherhood, elastic but unbreakable.

Jul 14, 2016 1:42pm

I'm out the door, on my way for the final days of Catskills Irish Arts Week. See ya!

Jul 27, 2016 10:47am

I don't wear hats.

But I've been thinking lately, I should cover my head when I'm out in the sun. So I bought a bandana and worked out how to tie a respectable do-rag.

The look suits me, and I'm much more comfortable in the hot sun. But there seems to be a side effect I hadn't anticipated.

In the grocery store yesterday, I encountered the same cashier I've seen often before, but without the do-rag.

"Hello, Darlin'," she said.

On the way out, the woman who had been ahead of me in line struck up a conversation.

"Hmmm ..." I thought. "Something's going on here."

Jul 30, 2016 6:14pm

Arleen: "It's too hot to read knitting magazines."

Aug 01, 2016 7:44am

Ryokan, a Zen master, lived the simplest kind of life in a little hut at the foot of a mountain. One evening a thief visited the hut only to discover there was nothing in it to steal.

Ryokan returned and caught him. "You may have come a long way to visit me," he told the prowler, "and you should not return empty-handed. Please take my clothes as a gift."

The thief was bewildered. He took the clothes and slunk away.

Ryokan sat naked, watching the moon. "Poor fellow, "he mused, "I wish I could give him this beautiful moon."

~ From Zen Flesh, Zen Bones, compiled by Paul Reps

Aug 5, 2016 1:28

Are you going to give me that thing or not?

Aug 10, 2016 12:35pm

A rather damp red-tailed hawk in the afternoon rain. I watched her with binoculars for a good long time. Spectacular image through the glasses. She watched me back through her spectacularly acute natural binocular eyes as I spoke to her softly, praising what a magnificent animal she is.

Aug 10, 2016 3:08pm

Amid the uproar over US Olympic gymnastics team member Gabby Douglas forgetting to put hand over heart for the national anthem, a friend from my hometown wrote:

"When your wife, daughter, mother or friend is raped and beheaded by a radical islamic terrorist who's friends with obama write me back and tell me how you feel then. This is America. Act like you respect our Country and quit making it OK to be wrong.

I replied:

You asked that I write you back when a family member or friend is executed by terrorists. It occurs to me, I owe you a response now.

In 1933, when my father was fifteen years old, my grandfather was thrown off a bridge in Rockford, Illinois. Murdered for the offense of being a Jew with plans to open a department store. The week my father's family moved to Rockford, during the night, someone painted JEW in big red letters across their front door. The people who murdered my grandfather likely considered themselves devout Christians.

They were terrorists.

My father went on to serve with distinction in WWII, which he considered his personal fight because of Hitler's program of exterminating the Jews.

We don't think much about domestic terrorism. When someone like Dylan Roof executes nine black people at church, the news media refer to him as a mentally unstable lone actor, not a terrorist. There is a long tradition of such white supremacist terrorism, including incidents like the 1963 Birmingham church bombing and the Philadelphia, Mississippi civil rights worker murders.

The teaching of history has been sanitized to tell that the great African-American migration from the South to the industrial cities of the north was "in search of opportunity." In reality, a great many black people fled the south to escape lynchings, beatings, and death threats. A black man could be murdered for so much as looking at a white woman.

The people who committed those terrorist acts in the South considered themselves Christians. They used their interpretation of the Bible to justify slavery and white supremacy.

Regarding the Ku Klux Klan, an American Christian domestic terrorist organization:

"After the American Civil War of 1861–1865, former Confederates and members of the Democratic Party organized the Protestant-led Ku Klux Klan (KKK) organization and began engaging in arson, beatings, destruction of property, lynching, murder, rape, tar-and-feathering, whipping and intimidation via such means as cross burning. They targeted African Americans, Jews, Catholics, and other social or ethnic minorities.

Vehemently anti-Catholic, Klan members had an explicitly Protestant Christian terrorist ideology, basing their beliefs in part on a 'religious foundation' in Protestant Christianity. The goals of the KKK included, from an early time onward, an intent to 'reestablish Protestant Christian values in America by any means possible', and they believed that 'Jesus was the first Klansman.' From 1915 onward, Klansmen conducted cross-burnings not only to intimidate targets, but also to demonstrate their respect and reverence for Jesus Christ, and the ritual of lighting crosses was steeped in Christian symbolism, including prayer and singing hymns. Within Christianity the Klan directed hostilities against Catholics. Modern Klan organizations remain associated with acts of domestic terrorism in the US." (Wikipedia)

And this about lynchings in the South:

"From 1882-1968, 4,743 lynchings occurred in the United States. Of these people that were lynched 3,446 were black. The blacks lynched accounted for 72.7% of the people lynched. These numbers seem large, but it is known that not all of the lynchings were ever recorded. Out of the 4,743 people lynched only 1,297 white people were lynched. That is only 27.3%. Many of the whites lynched were lynched for helping the black or being anti-lynching and even for domestic crimes .... .

Most of the lynchings that took place happened in the South. A big reason for this was the end of the Civil War. Once blacks were given their freedom, many people felt that the freed blacks were getting away with too much freedom and felt they needed to be controlled. Mississippi had the highest lynchings from 1882-1968 with 581. Georgia was second with 531, and Texas was third with 493."

Please note: "Of these people that were lynched 3,446 were black." That is more black people executed at the hands of extremist Christian American terrorists than all who died in the 9/11 attacks. Those are documented, PUBLIC murders of black citizens. How many more murders were not documented? There could have been ten times as many. My grandfather's execution is not included in that list. His was not a public murder and he was not black, but he died at the hands of white supremacist terrorists nonetheless.

http://www.chesnuttarchive.org/classroom/lynchingstat.html

Aug 12, 2016 10:13am

Here's the 21-speed mountain bike I brought home from the recycling transfer station two weeks ago.

It was missing a crank, needed a new chain, front brake pads, two spokes. I put a recycled kickstand on it. Alpina 501, when new in 1996 sold for $400. Nicest bike I've owned.

Aug 13, 2016 8:44pm

Over the past several days, I've been coming to terms with some facts about my family that I had only seen in pieces before.

Yesterday I did some reading about Ku Klux Klan activity in Illinois. I learned Rockford is in a part of the state where the Klan was intensely active during that era (and it appears, is still active to this day). It is almost certain the people who murdered my grandfather were Ku Klux Klansmen.

I would submit, in extremist Christian terror organizations like the Ku Klux Klan, American Christianity descended into similar patterns of doctrine and behavior as those we find reprehensible in extremist Muslim terror organizations. Perhaps we cannot, or will not, see this because it is too troubling to imagine "we" could be capable of the same kinds of barbarism as "they" are.

I do not believe it is religion itself that is at fault. Rather, people of all temperaments, whether holy or evil, will project their attitudes onto whatever spiritual teachings they find in their revered traditions.

Thus, you have the patient nonviolence of the Dalai Lama and the murderous militarism of WWII Japanese Zen Buddhism emerging from the same tradition.

You have the transcendent compassion and generosity of Sufism and the atrocities of Al Qaeda and ISIS emerging from the same tradition.

And you have the open-hearted benevolence of Pope Francis today (like his thirteenth century namesake, Saint Francis of Assisi), and the horrors of the twentieth century American Ku Klux Klan emerging from the same tradition.

In my opinion, it is not religion that corrupts man; it is man who corrupts religion.

Aug 14, 2016 7:08pm

Sixteen wild turkeys in the yard today. Twelve I've seen frequently together (two adult hens with their adolescent broods) and further down the hayfield, four adults I hadn't seen before.

Aug 15, 2016 11:08am

"Dear Mr. Freeman,

I'm writing to tell you how very happy I am with my Freeman-tweaked Whistle, a Blackbird in the key of D.

As the granddaughter of Irish immigrants, I've grown up surrounded by and loving Irish music. The tin whistle was always my favorite, so when I came across one in an Irish gift shop I bought it. Well, I'm sure you've heard this sort of thing before. Long story short, I found myself wondering if I was a musical disaster or if my whistle was a dud, and afraid to find out the hard way by saving up and buying a very expensive instrument that it was me. In the end, the only thing that stopped me from giving up entirely was finding out about your whistles.

I don't know what goes into the process of tweaking. I imagine it takes some time to perfect each whistle and you keep them affordable, so I doubt you're able to make much money on it. But there is a real need for whistles like yours. I cringe at the thought of children making their first venture into music with the same kind of whistle I started with. It'll seem to them that they can't get anywhere with a simple tin whistle, so why bother trying anything more complicated? What a sad thing that would be for music, not only for the discouragement of a few who are truly talented, but also for the average players. The ones who, like myself, play just for the wonderful pleasure of it.

Again, thank you for your craft. The Freeman Blackbird opened up a whole new world for me. It is the expression of joy, life, loss, love, and wonder, while also being a representative of my heritage and the music I love, all rolled into one of the sweetest-voiced instruments I've ever heard.

Sincerely,
S."

Aug 17, 2016 8:16am

I could use some moral support.

For the last several days, I've been ill with a severe flu. This morning my temp was 103 degrees F. This is problematic because I have adrenal insufficiency, which makes the flu particularly dangerous. It can trigger an adrenal crisis, which is life-threatening. I have a protocol that helps lessen the intensity of the illness, and I'm feeling better than I did a few hours ago, but I would appreciate your thoughts and prayers.

Update: 10:20 am, fever's down to 100.2, feeling MUCH better. Thanks for all your healing messages.

Update: 3:22 pm, fever's gone, feeling tired, but all's well. The danger of adrenal crisis has passed, thankfully. (It was a rough night.)

Update: 7:50 am Thursday, improved, to be sure, but I'm still sick. It's under control now, though. Not worrisome at this stage and comfortable most of the time.

Aug 19, 2016 9:45pm

Feeling better today. Awoke with some energy and ambition this morning, actually got some work done.

Aug 20, 2016 4:47pm

Congratulations to Iarla McMahon, 2014 under-12 Tin Whistle All-Ireland Champion, and now 2016 under-12 Uilleann Pipes All-Ireland Champion, as well!

And I know he's up against incredibly talented competition in this division. A great achievement.

Aug 23, 2016 4:47pm

I ordered heating oil. Today's price is $1.86/gallon. In past years it's been over three and even over four dollars per gallon.

When I finished placing the order I realized, this will be the first in many winters we will be able to afford to keep the house warm enough. I've been dreading the coming season, based on how we've suffered through the last fifteen or so.

What a relief that is.

Aug 25, 2016 9:45pm

Quote of the day: "We don't mess around with water."

Said by the plumber who had just replaced our failed well water tank, which had left the household dry.

Since it seemed to me, water is exactly what plumbers mess around with, I waited for him to elaborate, hoping to pick up his drift without having to say, "What do you mean, you don't mess around with water?"

"Anybody's water goes off, we're right on it," he said.

Aha. In fact, his boss showed up within an hour of my call and the workers arrived soon after. I was impressed.

Aug 26, 2016 7:19am

6:45 am, Sixteen wild turkeys outside my window. Max seems to understand I don't want him to bark at them. These are the same turkeys as the July 8 picture. Look how grown-up they are now!

Aug 30, 2016 4:30pm

I spent the morning at the retina specialist. The vision in my right eye has been deteriorating the last couple of years, started deteriorating faster in the last few months.

The good news is, if untreated, it won't be catastrophic, and there is a surgery that can repair the retinal hole, but it's best to do the surgery before the hole enlarges too much. Tentatively, I'll have the eye surgery in January, after the holiday season, which is the busiest for my whistle business.

The bad news is, though the surgery itself isn't especially traumatic, the recovery period is an ordeal.

The retina must be kept dry 24/7 for seven days after, and then at night and as much of the day as practical for the next seven days.

To accomplish that, the surgeon removes the fluid from inside the eyeball and fills it with sulfur hexafluoride gas to create a bubble that will rise to the top of the eyeball's interior. That requires "positioning" to keep the gas bubble against the retina at the back of the eyeball all the time.

In other words, I must be looking straight down, whether awake or asleep, twenty-four/seven.

I went through a less intensive period of positioning when I had emergency surgery for a detached retina in the other eye a few years ago. That was one of the toughest things I've been through. But at that time I was allowed to work by positioning myself face down above whatever I was working on. This time, I won't be allowed to move my eyes enough to work, so I'll be nearly 100% incapacitated.

Sep 01, 2016 7:57pm

Arleen came in with a mangled tuna fish can and a can opener. "YOU open it!" She said. "I can't get it to work."

I opened the can, showing her how you have to hold the can opener against the side of the can at the correct angle.

"Let me get this straight," I said. "You've got two advanced degrees, and I have to show you how to use a can opener. Didn't they teach you how to use a can opener in medical school?" She rolled her eyes, snatched the now opened tuna fish can from my hand and walked out.

Max had been next to me the whole time this was going on. He looked up expectantly. "There's nothing, Max," I said. "False alarm."

Max gave me his "What the hell?" look. He knew damn well there had been tuna fish, and he was demanding an explanation.

"OK, Max," I said. "How about this. Will this work?" I opened a drawer, took out a bottle of cod liver oil capsules and offered him one. He sniffed it briefly, picked it up delicately in his mouth and gazed at me appreciatively as he chewed the capsule.

Sep 02, 2016 7:44am

Max is barking his head off. Not only did a garbage truck drive by, it missed the turn and had to back up. "Holy shit, Max!" I said. "It's a garbage truck going backwards!"

Sep 09, 2016 7:02am

Looking out my window a few minutes ago, I saw our eleven resident wild turkeys meander across the driveway and take up station by the rose thicket.

Soon after, Natasha, Maria and Mahlet came out to wait for the school bus. Just now, spooked by the nearness of the children, several turkeys flew back across the driveway toward the hayfield. Max barked his head off. "Holy shit, Max," I said. "The turkeys can FLY!"

Sep 10, 2016 7:58am

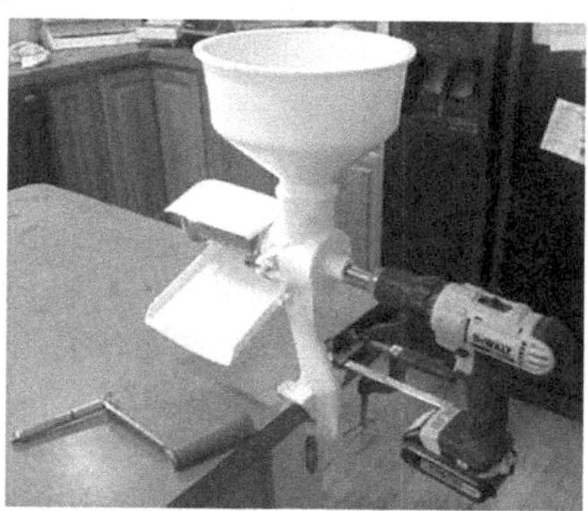

Well, I decided I'd had it with the Foley food mill I bought last year on the advice of a friend who cans a lot of tomatoes. Better than nothing, I guess, but still a lot of work.

So I ordered a Victorio Food Strainer Sauce Maker. It came in the mail day before yesterday. Used it the first time yesterday, and WOW! Boy that thing goes through tomatoes fast. You throw your whole tomatoes in the pot, get 'em good and cooked and then run them through the Victorio Food Strainer Sauce Maker and whammo! The skins and seeds come out the end and the sauce, nice and tidy, comes out the bottom. Then you put the sauce back on the stove and boil it down to however thick you want it.

Yesterday I picked the pear tree, brought in 80 pounds of Bosc pears. Last year, we put up 30 quarts of pear butter and everybody liked it. I'm thinking, this'll be a lot easier with the new Victorio Food Strainer Sauce Maker. But it's still going to be a lot of cranking the thing by hand.

I noticed you can buy an electric motor kit for more money than the Victorio Food Strainer Sauce Maker itself costs. No thanks. I've got a machine shop in the basement, should be able to motorize the Victorio Food Strainer Sauce Maker myself for free.

And I did ...

Sep 12, 2016 6:20pm

I'm pleased to report the Victorio Food Strainer Sauce Maker motorization project is an unqualified success. Today we put through six quarts of stewed tomatoes, on the way to boiling down to make sauce. Elapsed processing time through the (motorized!) Victorio Food Strainer Sauce Maker: 20 seconds.

<u>*Sep 13, 2016 7:46am*</u>

I wonder if I might ask for your help.

There is something important I'm trying to do and I need to raise some donations to be able to afford it.

You may know, the last three years I've been working on a book, *The Enlightenment Puzzle; A Practical Guide to Navigating the Truths and Fallacies About Awakening*. I'll post a draft of the introduction below. It's an ambitious project, and frankly, I expect it will be my only book.

There's still quite a bit to do, but it's coming along. There were several rather stubborn topics I'd been wrestling with for months and even years, and one by one they have fallen into place. Just in the last several weeks, I feel I finally have the entire book in hand.

In October the annual Science and Nonduality Conference will take place in San Jose, California. A few weeks ago, out of the blue, my friend Francis Bennett said, "I think you should come to SAND this year. I know someone who may be able to put you up so you won't have to stay in a hotel."

I don't know what I will find at the SAND conference, but I know it's important that I go. I'll be able to hear directly some of the well-known speakers about nonduality and awakening, and I'll be able to talk with them face to face. There will be conversations with writers, publishers, teachers, scholars, seekers and finders, all of which will help inform the writing.

When people ask, "How's the book coming?" I always tell them, "The book has a life of its own." And sometimes I tell them, "I'm not writing the book. The book is writing me." And so it seems.

Many of you know, my finances are always razor thin, and I've had to ask for help at times. Thankfully, the last year or two have been better, but I still have to scramble to pay the mortgage and keep the house heated. So I'm asking for your help again.

I have to tell you, your help and encouragement have been a godsend to me in so many ways. I treasure your friendship, and I am deeply grateful for your support. Truly, I can't imagine what my life would be like without you.

~~~~~~~~~~~~~~~~~~~~~~~~~~~

THE ENLIGHTENMENT PUZZLE
introduction (draft copy not for distribution)

At the core of every soul is an instinctual longing.

"Somewhere over the rainbow,
Way up high,
There's a land that I heard of
Once in a lullaby .... "

Everyone knows what "Over the Rainbow" is about. You feel the longing in your own soul and you connect with the universal instinct the song embodies.

Instincts are primordial. You may sense them, or you may not. You may be able to name them, or they may defy names. They urge you, they drive you, they compel you. Sometimes silently, sometimes quietly, sometimes intensely, sometimes violently.

No matter how we may congratulate ourselves that we are so advanced, that we are so civilized, instincts nonetheless rule. We deceive ourselves if we imagine otherwise.

To seek shelter and comfort, to forage, to couple and make new life, to nurture and protect, to discover and invent, to question and to teach .... And beyond all these, always there, always quietly urging us along, is one instinct, one desire, one longing ... to come home.

What is this longing? What, and where, is home? You could argue, that question motivates everything we humans do. Home is security. Home is acceptance. Home is comfort. Home is family. Home is peace.
~~~~~~~~~~~~~~~~~~~~~~~~~~~

Above all, home is peace. Every effort for anything, ultimately is motivated by the longing for peace. That is even true of striving after things that are intense, exciting, even violent. All striving is driven by a desire for satisfaction, for peace. When we finally are at peace, we are home.

OK, fine.

But what does it mean to be "finally at peace?"

That is the question we will explore in this book. There could be many answers, and I will not try to say that any one of them is the "right" answer. But I will tell you about AN answer that I believe provides a Rosetta Stone, a master map, for comprehending the breadth and extent of human experience that is called by such names as "awakening," "liberation," "Self-realization," "enlightenment."

In the Yoga, Vedanta, neo-advaita, non-dualism, etc. culture, there is much discussion, pro and con, point and counter-point, of "states," "stages," "levels" and "dimensions," of "awakening," "deepening" and "integration." Sometimes it seems people are talking about completely different realities and claiming their particular reality is THE awakening. It's confusing.

But all this, seemingly random and chaotic information actually fits a logical and comprehensible outline.

Understanding that outline, it becomes clear how the seemingly contradictory explanations and descriptions fit together. Because they do in fact, fit together. And that makes a huge difference for anyone who is looking for their own answers, their own peace, their own awakening, their own liberation, their own enlightenment.

As you go through this book, it will become clear why this is so. I will describe the different kinds of awakening, which give rise to different, apparently contradictory descriptions of what awakening is.

I will discuss the major truths and I will also discuss the major fallacies that are circulating in the culture today. I will discuss the practical ramifications of this knowledge, including recommendations how to evaluate your own practice, and how to better understand your own experience, your own awakening. And I will describe, clearly and comprehensively, what awakening is and how it unfolds. This will demonstrate, clearly and unmistakably, that the contradictory descriptions of awakening are in fact, not contradictory at all.

What I have to say here is not my own invention. I was fortunate to learn Transcendental Meditation when I was still eighteen years old, and to begin studying with Maharishi Mahesh Yogi before the age of twenty. I have continued in this meditation for over forty years now, and I've continued to study Maharishi's teachings right to this day. What I will say here is not an official presentation of Maharishi's teaching, as it includes numerous observations and conclusions that are my own. However, the great insights about awakening, the potential of human consciousness, enlightenment, etc. are not mine. They are Maharishi's.

****

Note: On August 21, 2017, as I was editing these pages, I felt compelled to write ...

"Somewhere over the rainbow,
Way up high,
There's a land that I heard of
Once in a lullaby ... ."

I happened upon those words just now, and they brought tears. Few know the story behind them.

Remember "Brother, Can You Spare a Dime?" the anthem of the Great Depression?

"Once I built a railroad, I made it run
Made it race against time
Once I built a railroad, now it's done
Brother, can you spare a dime?"

The lyrics were written by Edgar Yipsel "Yip" Harburg, who was born Isidore Hochberg in 1896. To have only written "Brother, Can You Spare a Dime?" would have secured Harburg's place as one of the greatest songwriters of all time. But he also wrote "Over the Rainbow," which remains to this day one of the most loved songs ever written.

What do you suppose prompted Harburg to write "Over the Rainbow's" immortal lyrics?

In 1939, during the making of *The Wizard of Oz*, Harburg was working as the movie's lyricist. Production was almost finished, and Harburg's work was wrapping up. At the same time, Hitler's project of persecuting Jews was running full throttle, and Harburg was heartbroken over the state of the world. The United States had turned its back to the plight of European Jews and did almost nothing to provide sanctuary, leaving millions to perish at the hands of Nazi exterminators.

He wrote his feelings into lyrics and put them aside.

Then, it occurred to him they might fit in the movie. He presented the idea to the producers, but they were against it. They said it was a sappy song, and it would slow down the story. But he did convince them to include "Over the Rainbow," and it became the most memorable song in the movie.

In the film, the lyrics are about a girl's longing for meaning in her life, but to the man who wrote them, they were about the plight of millions of Jews, stranded without rescue in the midst of the most brutal genocide in human history.

Nine days ago, Heather Heyer was murdered at a neo-Nazi rally in Charlottesville, Virginia by white supremacists promoting the same agenda that exterminated six million Jews in Europe (they also murdered my grandfather in Rockford, Illinois).

They organized through a website that ran stories calling for genocide, filled with swastikas and other Nazi symbols. The site was called "daily stormer dot com," invoking the German Nazi party's newspaper, Der Stürmer, which began calling for the extermination of Jews in 1933, the year my grandfather was murdered. The night before Heather Heyer's murder, hundreds of alt-right demonstrators carried torches across the University of Virginia campus, shouting "Blood and soil!" "Jews will not replace us!"

I'm in tears because what is happening now bears a terrifying resemblance to what was happening in the United States in 1939.

Again, we have turned our backs on millions of refugees who fled for their lives (not Jews this time, but Muslims), and again forces of hatred are claiming the world for a "master race."

Sep 14, 2016 10:21pm

Awhile back, I started wearing a bandana do-rag to keep from frying my scalp in the summer sun. And I noticed, women seem to respond in a different way when I'm wearing it.

I went to the grocery store, and the checkout woman I've seen a dozen times said, "Hello, Darlin'." Then another woman struck up a conversation on the way out of the store.

Later, as I was leaving the pharmacy with my prescription, the (female) cashier said, "Stay out of trouble!"

Today I was near the Salvation Army Store, so I thought I'd check and see if they had anything I could use. I found a fifty foot length of new garden soaker hose for $3.99 and a Hewlett Packard printer for $5.99. I like Hewlett Packard because I know how to refill the ink cartridges.

In the checkout line, the woman behind me said, "Nice hose," and we chatted about garden hoses. On the way out, I had to back through and push the door open with my butt because my hands were full. A woman coming in gave me a big smile and said, "I would have opened that for you!"

Sep 15, 2016 9:55am

Today's pickings. HUNDREDS more on the vine waiting for the intense heat to break so they can ripen.

Sep 16, 2016 5:00pm

Jim was here today working the hayfield. Usually, afterward, barn swallows circle and dart overhead.

Today, instead of barn swallows, there were four vultures. I got the binoculars and enjoyed a long, clear viewing of them, in flight (and close!) and walking around on the ground. Gorgeous birds in the air, dopey-looking cute on foot.

One of the birds had a red head, the other three had gray heads. At first, I thought the gray-headed ones might be black vultures, but the wing markings were clearly turkey vulture. A little online reading, and I learned the gray-headed vultures are juvenile birds.

So what I saw was a family outing. Mom and her three kids.

Sep 24, 2016 9:25am

We have three dogs – Max, Antoine and Isabella. Mostly I write about Max. This post is about Antoine, who is a ten-pound, miniature English poodle.

Antoine is a very polite dog. Just now, the kitchen table is covered, edge to edge, with tomatoes we will can in the next couple of days. Antoine likes to eat tomatoes.

I came down to the kitchen and found one of the chairs had been left out from the table. Antoine could jump up and get to the tomatoes.

And there he was. I watched awhile as Antoine carefully sniffed one tomato, then carefully sniffed the next tomato, then carefully sniffed the next tomato. He did this a long time, sniffing every tomato he could reach. Looking closely, I saw he hadn't eaten any at all. Such a polite dog.

It occurs to me, with Antoine's help, we could count the tomatoes. It would go something like this:

"Here's a tomato. And here's another tomato! And another tomato. And another tomato. And another tomato ... ." Antoine is good at counting tomatoes.

Sep 30, 2016 9:52am

Turkey firearm season starts tomorrow.

"Half to three fourths of each season's poults will not survive their first year of life. ... Turkeys that survive their first year, though, have little to fear from any predator (except humans) and can live up to 15 years in their natural habitats."

Last I counted, there are eight turkeys. That would be two hens and six, now grown, poults. Hens lay 10 to 12 eggs, so there would have been around 22 hatchlings between the two broods.

I've been thinking, I need to train these birds to spend more time on our property where they won't be hunted. But how to do it?

Three years ago, our elderly neighbors, the Judkins, moved to Arizona to live with their daughter. Dan Judkins came over a couple of months before the move and told me he had some 30-year-old, 55-gallon drums of grain and powdered milk in his basement he needed to dispose of, and did I think I could use them?

I said I'd think about it, and I asked, "How do you happen to have them?" He explained that when the end of days comes, there will be droughts and famines. The elect will survive, but there will be nothing to eat except for what has been stored away. Thirty years ago, his church organized to make sure everyone in the congregation was prepared.

I stored the barrels under the deck. But I couldn't open them because the area under the deck wasn't dry. So they sat for three years until this summer, when I contrived a drainage system that carries away whatever rainwater falls between the deck boards.

"I can feed the grain to the turkeys," I thought, and worked out where to put the grain to lead them to safety.

This morning, I opened the barrels and found cracked wheat and whole grain rice. I set the mower cutting height all the way down and scalped a path from the driveway to the area alongside the garden enclosure, where the turkeys already spend a lot of time. And I tossed the grain along the path.

We'll see how it goes. (C'mon, girls.)

Note: For the next couple of weeks, I heard frequent gunfire, some of it relentless, repeated shots. I have not seen a single turkey on this property since.

Today (summer, 2017) I phoned the Connecticut Department of Wildlife Management. I asked, what was the tally of wild turkeys taken in the fall 2016 season? "Sixty," the man said. "It isn't a popular season because there's so much other hunting around then." He admitted there was unlicensed hunting that doesn't get counted but was skeptical that hunters could have taken my whole flock.

I looked at the state game website and found the hunting seasons for most species started later than the start of turkey season, typically two weeks after I'd heard most of the shooting. I remember a conversation with Roland, the farmer on the land next to ours. He referred to a neighbor, whose name I don't recall, who "shoots a lot of turkeys." I'm inclined to think he hunts without a license, but I'm not going to look into it.

There were no wild turkeys in Connecticut from the early 1800's to the 1970's, when repopulation efforts began to take hold. Today there are an estimated 35,000 to 40,000. I expect to see them again.

Oct 07, 2016 7:28pm

"I do absolutely LOVE the Blackbird whistle I got from you recently. Sweeeeet and plays so effortlessly. It's like pouring liquid melodies. I am a convert to your whistles and would love to now place a large order ... ."

Oct 07, 2016 8:48pm

The garden in October ...

Oct 10, 2016 10:19pm

Frost warning tonight. We covered the chard and picked the butternut squash (15 of them). We picked all the tomatoes with any color at all, to finish ripening indoors. And we picked the last watermelons (24 of them). It's sad to think, after eating watermelons every day for the last several weeks, there are only 24 left.

Oct 12, 2016 8:53pm

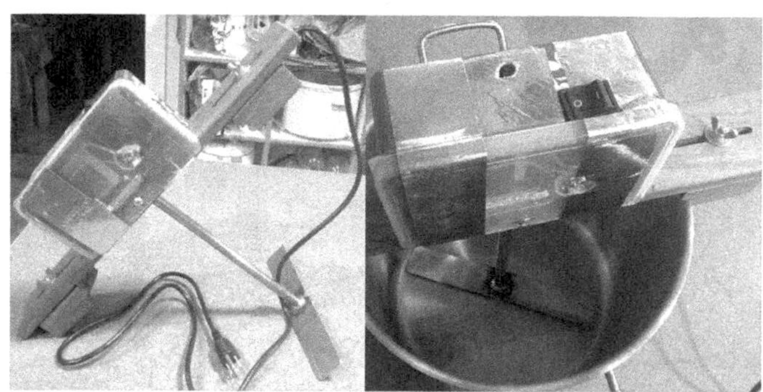

The motorized pot stirrer is complete. This will save a lot of time and a lot of work when we make tomato sauce, pear sauce, watermelon syrup, etc.

Oct 13, 2016 11:08am

OK, everybody. Stand back! The motorized pot stirrer is operational. Trying it out now on a batch of watermelon syrup ...

Oct 14, 2016 5:05pm

I want to express my heartfelt thanks to all who donated to help cover my expenses for the trip to the Science and Nonduality Conference beginning a few days from now. I'm deeply touched by your kind generosity. Again, thanks from the bottom of my heart.

Oct 15, 2016 5:42pm

I'm making another batch of watermelon syrup. The motorized pot stirrer is working great. What a wonderful labor-saving device! I just want to sit there and watch it swirl 'round and 'round for hours at a time.

<u>*Oct 17, 2016 8:25am*</u>

Max is barking his head off. "What is it, Max?" I asked. I looked out the window and saw a public works pickup truck with flashing yellow lights stopped in front of our mailbox. OUR mailbox!

"Holy shit, Max!" I said. "They can't do that. It's outrageous!"

<u>*Oct 17, 2016 2:36pm*</u>

Well, this situation has gotten completely out of hand. Max is very upset. Now there are BICYCLES going by. And the people riding them are wearing PINK SHIRTS! (Can dogs see pink?)

<u>*Oct 19, 2016 11:36am*</u>

I had a good flight, am settled where I'll be staying. Again, heartfelt gratitude to all who have made this possible for me.

<u>*Oct 19, 2016 7:10pm*</u>

My gracious California hostess

<u>*Oct 21, 2016 12:01pm*</u>

"Can I please eat your breakfast?"

Oct 27, 2016 11:43am

I got home from the Science and Nonduality conference around 1:00 this morning. Max is asleep on my bed, and there's still a watermelon from the garden, of the three that were on the table when I left. Life is good.

Oct 27, 2016 2:45pm

Sacked out

Nov 05, 2016 9:54am

"But they that wait upon the Lord shall renew their strength; they shall mount up with wings as eagles; they shall run, and not be weary; and they shall walk, and not faint."

Nov 06, 2016 8:37am

Just now I was taking some medicine. Max trotted in, perched his nose on my knee and looked up expectantly. "Hi, Max," I said. "It's not something to eat." Instantly, he spun around and trotted out. "Hmmm ..." I thought. "Max knows what that means. I must say it a lot."

Nov 06, 2016 11:41am

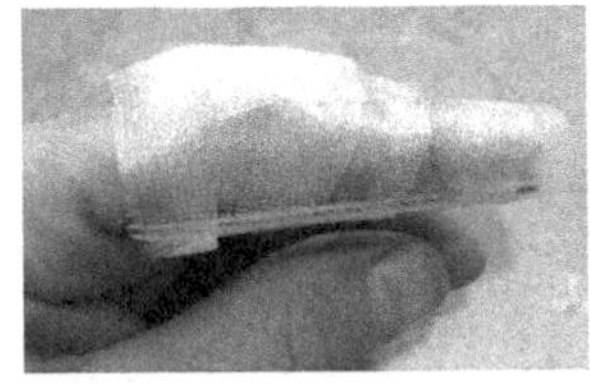

Today's good news ... no tendon damage. (Should be good as new in a week or two.) I get a lot of little cuts and burns and scrapes. This one's a little worse than most, but still not too bad.

<u>*Nov 06, 2016 12:35pm*</u>

The world as we knew it has ended.

Because it's hard to type, I'm trying out Google docs' "microphone typing" feature. I dictated the word "discovers," and it typed "discover's." I tried again, and again it typed "discover's." I tried to think of a sentence in which "discover's" would be a correct spelling. I couldn't think of a single one. Can you?

<u>*Nov 06, 2016 5:28pm*</u>

I'm beginning to use Google docs' "microphone typing" feature to transcribe an interview I did a few years ago. Some interesting attempts by the software to interpret my dictation:

"I'm going to base this in material that may be familiar to people that have some background in Nevada or Yoga orthodontist traditions."

And ...

"The nature of deep sleep is that the senses are asleep, the mind is asleep and the body is basically a nerd."

<u>*Nov 07, 2016 6:33pm*</u>

Max likes to play tug-of-war/throw-the-thing/maybe-I'll-bring-it-back/maybe-I-won't.

It always ends the same way. The thing is over there where I threw it and Max is over here looking up at me expectantly. "Sorry, Max. YOU have to bring it back."

<u>*Nov 09, 2016 12:09pm*</u>

Ours is not the struggle of a day, a week, a month, or a year – it is the struggle of lifetime. We must build a world at peace with itself.

~ *John Lewis*

<u>*Nov 10, 2016 10:42pm*</u>

"I understand the wounds
That have not healed in you.
They exist
Because God and Love
Have yet to become real enough
To allow you to forgive
The dream."

~ *Hafez*

Nov 11, 2016 8:38am

I woke up this morning feeling angry.

Whenever I wake up feeling angry or sad, I ask myself, "Why am I angry?" or "Why am I sad?" I'll find the reason and I'll think, "OK. That's why." The anger or sadness will dissolve, sometimes a little, sometimes completely.

This morning I asked myself, "Why am I angry?" I thought. "The election. Of course."

That perception led me back across a sweep of territory I've been pondering these last months and years:

Donald Trump is president because of slavery.

He lost the popular vote as did George W. Bush, Benjamin Harrison, Rutherford B. Hayes and John Quincy Adams, but he won the Electoral College.

In recent elections, it seems the consequences of this disparity have become increasingly dire.

What would have happened if Albert Gore Jr. (who won the popular vote) had become president instead of George W. Bush?

Certainly, we would not have invaded Iraq. There would be no ISIS, which emerged in the aftermath of that disastrous blunder. We might even have thwarted the 9/11 attacks, if President Gore had taken CIA warnings more seriously than President Bush did.

Perhaps there would not be wildfires in California; rising seas menacing Florida, Bangladesh and the world's island nations; torrential rains raising floodwaters in Louisiana and Texas; droughts and famines triggering sectarian civil wars in Syria and Sudan. Perhaps the world would not be in turmoil because millions of refugees have been driven from their homes by war and drought and famine.

The Electoral College system of choosing our president, created to protect slavery, has had a tremendously destructive impact on the United States and indeed the entire world. The great Sin of Our Fathers has been, and continues to be, visited upon us, the sons and daughters.

Before I went to bed last night, it occurred to me, "This election and what will come from it are like a movie, a really GRIPPING movie."

With that, I relaxed a bit. Children don't know movies aren't real. I was traumatized, as were many other four- and five-year-olds of the time, when the hunter killed Bambi's mother. "It's just a MOVIE." "It isn't REAL." "It didn't really

HAPPEN." "It's a STORY," mothers across America pleaded to their wailing sons and daughters.

But this is not a movie. It's real. It really did happen, and it really is happening. And it is not happening in the abstract, on a movie screen or in the pages of a book. It is happening here and now, and it is happening to US.

Still, I took some consolation. That sense, that what is happening is like a really gripping movie script, allowed me to feel enough distance to be able to see a little more widely, breathe a little more deeply.

How do we endure such times as these? Not by withdrawing, but also, not by being so overwhelmed we lose our ability to think clearly, to act powerfully.

So perhaps I'll use that sense, that this is like a really gripping movie, to let myself feel optimistic even when things get really dark, as I believe they well may do in the next few years. We don't know the ending yet. We don't know yet whether this movie is about the end of the world or the end of deadlocked, establishment politics and the beginning of a better world.

Nov 12, 2016 10:05pm

A guy goes to the doctor with a carrot in one ear, a stalk of celery in the other ear, an olive in one nostril. The doctor looks at him and says, "Man ... you're not eating right."

Nov 13, 2016 10:54am

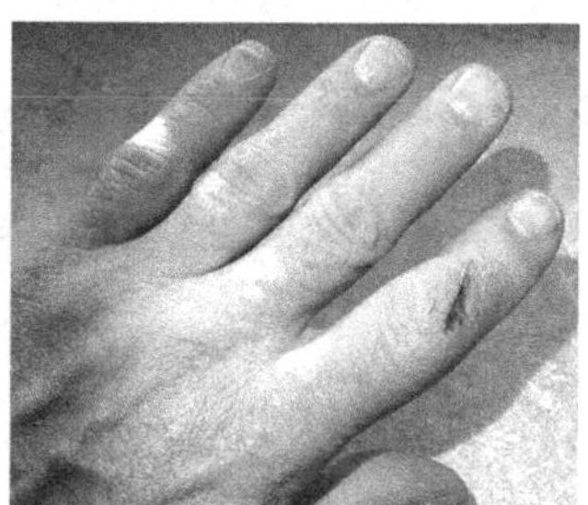

I had my first-ever acupuncture treatment Thursday. Dr. Koo's English is hard to understand, but we managed nonetheless.

"You indoors, right? Not outside, right?"

"No, I'm outside a lot."

"Inside. Not outside, right?"

"No, I'm outside a lot. I have a garden. I do a lot of outside work."

"Show hands!"

I held out my hands on his desktop.

"OK, OK. Outside."

Nov 18, 2016 11:56am

Hey, folks.

I've been debating whether to post this. So many people are demoralized right now. So what if I'm having a hard time myself?

But I am having a hard time. Despite all the years of meditation and whatever awakening has come along the way, my brain chemistry tends toward depression. This has been a delicate balance all my life (I attempted suicide twice as a teenager), but for the most part I've learned to feed the neurotransmitters what they need to keep the episodes tolerable and mostly brief.

Usually the main note in my experience is overflowing joy, but occasionally, circumstances or physiology tip the scale to the other side. I wrote an essay about it, which I've posted a few times and will again below.

For the last twenty-five or so years, I've also lived with Chronic Fatigue Syndrome, which I've been able to manage pretty well. There are some fairly severe limitations to the work I am able to do (which is why I'm chronically short of money, in case you've ever wondered), but I've created a business that allows me to function within those constraints.

The trip to California at the end of last month for the Science and Nonduality Conference was the first I'd traveled beyond driving distance in more than twenty years. The trip was wonderful, but I came back exhausted. I expected to recover my energy within a few days, but three weeks later I'm still exhausted and struggling to get any work done. I'm disappointed to discover, after all the work to rebuild my strength over the last two decades, I'm still too fragile to travel.

I'm sorry to bother you with such a gloomy post, but I need your support. I'm pretty isolated here. Most of the people I consider my friends are a distance away and I mainly connect with them (you) online.

Nov 18, 2016 11:58am

Suffering and nectar ...

In much Eastern spiritual and popular nondual Western culture, there's a tenet that says all suffering ceases when one awakens to a deeper Reality. There are statements of this in Eastern scripture, and it is often repeated in nondual discussions.

In fact it is true for some, for whom all suffering does end upon awakening. However, it is not universally true, and the expectation that life will be entirely without suffering can create problems.

When anyone attempts to evade genuine pain, believing such pain is incompatible with the awakening they seek, they can get sidetracked in aversion, often to the extent of unhealthy spiritual bypassing that denies the reality of whatever they are experiencing.

In so doing, they suppress parts of themselves and prevent them from becoming fully integrated into their awakening. So they remain divided within themselves, even in the effort to become enlightened. That is exactly the opposite of enlightenment, which must be whole and fully integrated.

Not all suffering is caused by delusion about Reality. Some is caused by organic forces that have nothing to do with one's level of awakening or non-awakening.

Especially, these may include patterns of brain chemistry or nerve signaling that cause intense psychic or physical pain. In the awakened person, these will fall in the category of "prarabhdha karma," the flow of karmas, both bodily and circumstantial, that have already begun to bear fruit and will necessarily play out in their lives. This may be true even though the person has awakened to a higher level of consciousness that has "burned the seeds" of karmas that have not yet begun to bear fruit.

In the awakened person there is a transcendental dimension that is beyond whatever pain there is. However, in some instances, the pain may be sufficiently intense, it can only be honestly characterized as suffering.

There is a further difference in the way a deeply awakened person experiences suffering. In the moment, that suffering may seem to contradict the sense that "all things are as they should be." However, because the awakened person sees reality from a more expansive viewpoint, his or her relationship to the pain or suffering will be quite different, and as a result, the outcome will be different.

"Without undue attachment or aversion to anything," a mature awakening will naturally release undue attachment or aversion to both pleasure and pain. Because all experiences are received with an evenness of attitude, suffering will not be compounded and prolonged because of one's reactions to it. And of course, there will still always remain a healthy attitude that naturally avoids unnecessary pain and gravitates to what is most joyful and fulfilling.

"The enlightened knower of Brahman drinks nectar from every particle of the universe," whether the first taste of each particle is bitter or sweet.

Whereas before, the bitter taste of pain was wounding and diminishing, in the wholeness of Brahman consciousness, "all things work for good." Because the deeply awakened knower of Reality processes experience differently, that bitterness transmutes in some sense into healing medicine or the pangs of creative birth.

The bitterness ultimately transforms to nectar when it has been fully assimilated and metabolized. So from time to time, there may be suffering in the moment, but in the greater scope of an awakened life, all experience, whether of pleasure or pain, is transformed to a deeper joyfulness that transcends relative joy and sorrow. In that respect, such an awakened person has indeed gone "beyond suffering."

So it's true, as both scripture and popular spiritual culture teach, that awakening to a higher reality is the solution to suffering. However, in practical experience, that does not always mean suffering itself disappears entirely and forever.

It bears mention here, Buddha never said life in the world is suffering, and he never said awakening, or nirvana, is the end of all suffering. What Buddha said was, life in the world is DUKKHA, which means life in the world is incapable of bringing satisfaction. And he said awakening, or nirvana, is the end of dukkha. So there may be what we could call suffering after awakening, but it will be different because after awakening, life will be meaningful, satisfying, in a way it could not have been before.

Nov 22, 2016 3:06pm

This means nothing to you, but it means a great deal to me. This morning, after weeks of strategizing how to get my 1944 machinist lathe to cut a precise 1.8184 degree taper (Jacobs 33) on a 5/8 inch steel rod, I completed the task. Perfectly. I thought, "If I can do that, I can probably handle the rest of what I'm dealing with."

This will be the new spindle for a beautiful 1950's era benchtop drill press I rescued from the recycling transfer station dumpster a couple of years ago. A drill press chuck is not held in place by any fastener. It fits so perfectly, it takes a heavy mallet blow to remove it. The next step will be to duplicate the slots in the other end of the spindle. (The old spindle is shown.)

Nov 22, 2016 10:52pm

Maria said, "You know what I don't like about Max? He wakes me up at two in the morning. He jumps out of my bed, leaves my room, goes to the top of the stairs and then turns back around and goes to your room."

I laughed and laughed.

That means I'm Max's second choice (third if you count Maria's bed). Max's first choice is the kitchen. He goes to the stairs to check if anyone's in the kitchen, where there is FOOD. "No one's in the kitchen. Damn. I'll just go to Jerry's room then."

Nov 26, 2016 5:50pm

Homework

Nov 27, 2016 1:26pm

Hard time of the year for a lot of folks. Suicide Hotline is 800-273-TALK (8255). Trans Lifeline is a trans-specific resource along the same lines. US: (877) 565-8860 Canada: (877) 330-6366. Also Veteran's Crisis line, which is for Vets, their family and friends, is 800-273-8255 and Press 1.

Nov 30, 2016 7:46pm

"Max," I said, "the human throws the thing and the dog brings it back. Remember?"

"Huh?" says Max, looking up expectantly.

<u>*Dec 01, 2016 3:35pm*</u>

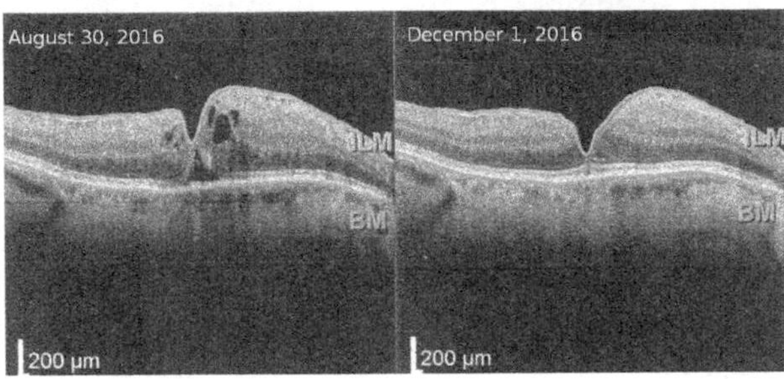

Here's a miracle for you ....

In August, my eye surgeon said I'd need an operation to repair a hole in the macula of my right eye.

You can see the hole in the August 30 image, which is a cross section of the central part of the back of the eye. The hole is the black triangle at the bottom of the indentation in the middle (the indentation is normal). The black areas to the left and right of the indentation are also abnormal lesions.

That was August 30, right before I started bringing in watermelons from the garden. Over the next two months, I ate forty watermelons, some directly from the garden and some as watermelon syrup, which I put in jars when there were too many watermelons to eat fresh. As it happens, watermelons have even more eye-nourishing lycopene than tomatoes.

Look at today's image of the same eye. My eye surgeon was amazed and he said so. Macular holes don't often heal by themselves. The best I'd hoped to hear was "It's stable, so we can watch it awhile before we have to do the operation."

But he said, "Well, it looks like we won't have to operate after all." I told him about the watermelons. I suggested he hand out packets of watermelon seeds to all his patients.

Hallelujah.

Note: On August 11, 2017, I saw my eye surgeon again. The macula shows no change from last visit, and my eyesight (with glasses) has improved to 20/20 in both eyes.

I've thought about the remarkable synchronicity of that watermelon crop.

I didn't know, when I was eating all those melons, that I needed a massive dose of lycopene to heal my eye. And I didn't know, when I planted them, that watermelon is one of the richest sources. In fact, when I planted the watermelons, I didn't even know there was something wrong with my eye.

My sense however, is someone DID know. I was reminded again that we humans can only know one thing at a time, and then only in terms of past, present and future. But past and future exist simultaneously in God's vision, who knows all things at once and organizes them with sublime synchronicity. God arranges every detail, for each of us, personally, perfectly, even when we ourselves do not see it.

Dec 10, 2016 7:51am

The Sunrise Ruby

In the early morning hour, just before dawn, lover and beloved awake and take a drink of water.

She asks, Do you love me or yourself more? Really, tell me the absolute truth.

He says, There is nothing left of me. I am like a ruby held up to the sunrise. Is it still a stone, or a world made of redness? It has no resistance to sunlight. The ruby and the sunrise are one. Be courageous and discipline yourself.

Work. Keep digging your well. Don't think about getting off from work. Submit to a daily practice. Your loyalty to that is a ring on the door.

Keep knocking, and the joy inside will eventually open a window and look out to see who's there.

~ Jalāl ad-Dīn Muhammad Rūmī

Dec 15, 2016 10:16pm

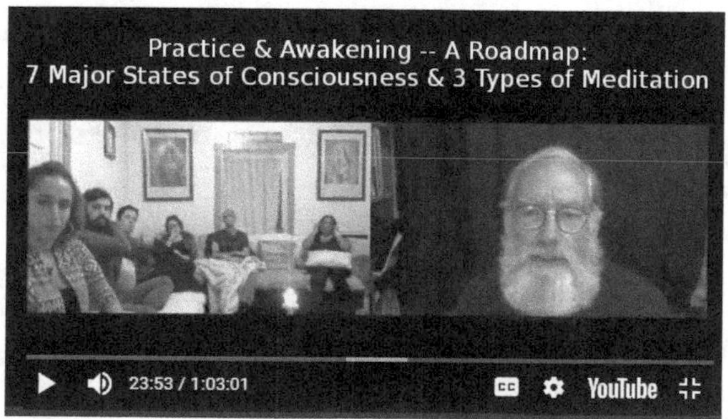

Here's the presentation I made to the Urban Awakening group Sunday evening

Dec 16, 2016 7:36am

As I sit here eating a pomegranate, Max is begging with all his canine enthusiasm. He LOVES pomegranates, begs for them more intensely than I've seen him beg for any other treat. He must have been reading about antioxidants.

<u>*Dec 17, 2016 7:47am*</u>

"Shall we expect some transatlantic military giant, to step over the ocean, and crush us at a blow? Never! – All the armies of Europe, Asia and Africa combined, with all the treasure of the earth (our own excepted) in their military chest; with a Bonaparte for a commander, could not by force, take a drink from the Ohio, or make a track on the Blue Ridge, in a trial of a Thousand years. At what point, then, is the approach of danger to be expected? I answer, if it ever reach us, it must spring up amongst us. It cannot come from abroad. If destruction be our lot, we must ourselves be its author and finisher. As a nation of freemen, we must live through all time, or die by suicide."

~ *Abraham Lincoln*

<u>*Dec 23, 2016 5:45pm*</u>

I'm teaching Max not to bark so much. This is complicated because he has to bark and then I have to get him to stop barking and then I have to reward him for stopping.

He's getting the idea. Sometimes when he wants to bark, he just makes polite little "Ahem" noises, for which I reward him immediately.

And sometimes he does bark out loud. Then if he stops barking on command, he gets a reward.

However, sometimes he barks out loud for no apparent reason, then stops barking immediately. He looks at me and licks his chops. "I stopped barking. Where's my treat?"

Sigh. I can't reward that because it would put the cart before the horse, so to speak. If I reward him when he does that, Max will have trained me to give him treats on command.

<u>*Dec 25, 2016 7:51pm*</u>

Max can get more "likes" in a few hours than I can get in a week. My only advantage is, Max can't type.

<u>*Dec 25, 2016 10:55pm*</u>

I've lost track of how this training thing is supposed to work. If I don't bark, I'm supposed to give Max a treat, right?

Dec 30, 2016 8:48pm

As far as I can tell ...

There's nothing but God no matter where you look. Anything that seems outside God's domain only seems that way as a transitional appearance.

My experience has been, anything in my life that seems to clash or draw my attention "away" from God is only something in which I've not yet fully seen Her.

When I allow myself to see into whatever thing seems "distracting," I come to terms with it and I discover that She is and always was in the midst of it. Then I find, there's that much more of Her and the little "me" is that much less bewildered.

In this there is an alchemy that turns all dross to gold and all bitterness to nectar. The sense is, God is hiding behind everything that seems to contradict Her. And She hides there INTENTIONALLY, only to reveal Herself again and again in places I would not have thought to look for Her. In this, She is allowing me to see more and more of Her, as long as I remain faithful to that process by which She continually allows me to find Her.

2017

Jan 01, 2017 7:57pm

Here's the ~80-year-old drill press I salvaged a couple of years ago. It had been discarded because the spindle taper was galled beyond repair and the motor was worn out. The restoration is complete.

I made a new spindle, which required working out how to cut a Jacobs 33 taper on my lathe and milling six slots for it to engage the drive pulley. Those two operations took a couple of years to figure out and execute.

I replaced the bearings and return spring, made or refurbished various other parts and installed a nice chuck.

It needed a motor. In my collection I found a washing machine motor of the right speed and horsepower. Maytag, so it's a good one. It needed a mounting bracket, so I fashioned a new one from suitable steel.

The motor is whisper quiet. I bought it for five dollars from one of my Amish friends back in rural New York. The washing machine it came from, he'd converted to run off a lawn mower motor.

Jan 07, 2017 8:26am

At the junction of waking and dreaming, sometimes the two states of consciousness intermix and my awake mind reflects on what my dreaming mind encounters.

Yesterday morning just before dawn, I saw in my dream a squadron of skaters rolling down our hill. Then my waking mind heard the snowplow, which sounded like twenty children on the steel-wheeled skates we had when I was a boy.

"How is it," I thought, "that my dreaming mind saw the moving scene of skaters before I could actually hear the sound that image arose from?"

Jan 13, 2017 11:05am

When Max begs for food without success, he'll walk around to the other side and try again. "If the human doesn't respond when I beg on the left, maybe he'll respond if I beg on the right." Logical, worth a try.

Jan 16, 2017 2:13pm

"Why they call it 'the Irish pipe organ'"

Max, who had never heard uilleann bagpipes before, was also impressed. He growled at it, suppressing the impulse to bark. Then he turned around and walked out.

Half a minute later he came back in and stood across the room with a concerned look in his eye. When the music was finished, he came over and requested his reward for not barking at the Irish pipe organ. Clearly, a memorable experience for Max.

Jan 18, 2017 9:25pm

"A lot of people want to serve God, but only in an advisory capacity."

Jan 22, 2017 9:14pm

Often, there's a single piece of toast in the toaster.

Arleen makes toast for herself and then gets sidetracked. A lot. This evening, she was doing something in the kitchen. I told her I needed the cable provider's password so I could watch something on my computer. "OK," she said, "I'll go upstairs and look it up. But if I forget my toast it will be your fault."

Arleen began looking through her notebooks to find where she'd written the password. "While I'm here, why don't I set up the antivirus software on your new laptop," I said.

She continued to search for the password while I worked on the computer. "Here it is!" she said. It took several minutes longer to get the antivirus software installed. I handed her the laptop and showed her a few things. Then I left to go back to my office.

Halfway down the hall, I remembered why I'd followed Arleen upstairs.

I went back to Arleen and said, "How about this? I'll trade you your piece of toast for the password."

Jan 23, 2017 1:46pm

Do I dare post this?

Max barked for no apparent reason. I "shooshed" him and he quieted down. But I don't like to reward him with treats unless he barks at an obvious provocation and then stops on command. I don't want to teach him he can get treats by barking for no other reason than he wants a treat.

So I petted him and praised him for quieting down when I asked him to. He rolled on his back to signal he wanted a tummy rub. "You like tummy rubs, don't you, Max?" I said. "Probably because you can't rub your tummy yourself. I can rub my tummy, see? There are some advantages to being a human." I thought about that for a second. "But then, I can't lick my ... Oh, never mind."

Jan 30, 2017 10:38pm

Lately Max has been spending a lot of time online. He's been saying "WTF!?!" (He thinks it means "Where's the food!?!")

Feb 05, 2017 5:12pm

"I am empty of everything and there is nothing left in my mind," said the monk to Joshu. "What do you say to that?"

Joshu said, "Cast that away."

But the monk persisted. "I have told you, there is nothing left in me. I am completely empty. What can I cast away?"

"In that case," replied Joshu, "keep on carrying it."

Feb 11, 2017 6:23pm

I'm so excited I can hardly stand it! My DIODE arrived in the mail today. This is no ordinary diode. It's a fifty-amp, six-hundred-volt button diode, very hard to find. God willing, it will make my MIG welder work again after ten years. How did I ever survive without my welder?

Feb 11, 2017 9:20pm

Max got his bangs trimmed!

Feb 13, 2017 5:55pm

As you know, with my help Max has been working on the finer points of barking etiquette. He's figured out that barking to notify the humans of something important is acceptable, but barking just for fun is frowned upon.

Just now, I took a break from my work to catch a quick nap. Max, with his super dog senses, monitors the status of every bed in the house. Within a minute or two, he appears from nowhere and jumps into any bed newly occupied by a human being. I greeted Max when he arrived and settled down to rest.

Somewhere between drowsy waking consciousness and dream consciousness, the words "Are you ready?" passed through my mind. "Yeah," I thought, now more awake than asleep. Instantly, Max jumped up and ran out of the room, barking at something in another part of the house.

"How did he do that?" I asked myself.

Feb 14, 2017 5:10pm

One of my favorite things ever! It seems the Atlanta Zoo had a bet with a zoo in Rhode Island that whoever lost the Superbowl would have to name one of their baby animals after the winning quarterback. The Atlanta zoo now has a baby Madagascar hissing cockroach named Tom Brady.

Feb 23, 2017 9:10pm

Me: "Come back. I have one more thing to show you." (YouTube video)

Arleen: "I can't. I have to find out who murdered the clown." (Father Brown)

Feb 24, 2017 1:49pm

Arleen: "Call Isabella."

Me: "You're competing with a sunbeam."

Arleen: "Never mind."

Feb 25, 2017 7:38pm

In case you were wondering, Arleen did find out who murdered the clown. It wasn't who you would have expected, she told me.

Feb 26, 2017 5:39pm

My neighbor Jim told me, "Women are SO impatient. You tell them you'll do something, and for some reason they think they have to remind you every six months."

Mar 02, 2017 9:13am

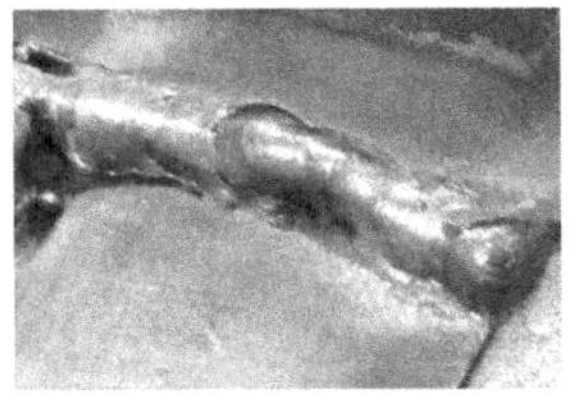

Ladies and gentlemen, the welder is back! After ten years

Mar 04, 2017 6:53am

Max does not bark at random cars going by.

This evening, a friend of Maria's was coming for a sleepover. Suddenly, Max started barking. From my office window, I can see far down the road. I looked up to find out what he might have been responding to, but no vehicles were in sight.

Then, out of the distance, a car came into view. As it drew closer, it slowed down, and then it turned into the driveway. Max knew it was coming before I could see it. AND he knew it was coming to our house! As I said, Max doesn't bark at random cars. He only barks at cars that come to our house.

I'm beginning to wonder how many more things he knows that are beyond human comprehension.

Mar 08, 2017 7:07am

Middle of the night, sound asleep. Max is sleeping at the foot of the bed. On the movie screen of dream consciousness I see a 1950's pen-and-ink cartoon of a man's face with a surprised expression. A "startled" icon. A split second later, Max barks. "What just happened?" I ask myself.

Mar 08, 2017 8:25am

After weeks of puzzling out ways to get to the top of our chimney more than forty feet up, to place a stainless steel flue liner for the wood burning fireplace insert I'm installing, I decided the only safe way would be to set up scaffolding and anchor it to the masonry. I could rent it a week for around $325, or I could try to find it on Craigslist and buy it.

What you see on my utility trailer is:

6 - 10' aluminum planks
8 - casters
11 - leveling jacks (I can replace the missing one for $22.50)
16 - 10' cross braces
2 - 48" X 60" frames
14 - 60" X 60" frames

If purchased new: $3250.00
I paid $600. My neighbor will pay half and store them on his farm.

My cost: $300, and I have scaffolding whenever I need it.

Mar 10, 2017 4:00pm

Max has been reading *The Power of Now*. Whenever anyone has food, he wants to know, "Can I have it NOW?"

Mar 10, 2017 7:25pm

Talking dirty ...

When I kiss Arleen in front of Antoine, he barks.

I whisper, "I can make your dog bark."

Mar 11, 2017 8:55pm

Lately I have been swaying along the boundary between life and death ...

I'm not terminally ill, not suicidal, but somehow circumstances have placed me in that arid territory. Much of the time lately I've been gazing across the veil toward the other side, which often seems close at hand, or looking back toward the world from a position where I seem to have no foothold in it. For months, and even years, I've been quietly puzzling how I might navigate this thin terrain and where I might find solid ground. In the last few weeks, the situation has been especially acute.

I'm tired. Twenty plus years with Chronic Fatigue Syndrome. I've helped raise nine children, three of whom are still living with us. Most days I have to stop and rest, hoping to get a second wind so I can make headway against a seeming mountain of unfinished, often urgent, tasks. There just isn't enough of me left for what the world is asking, and I don't know how to keep going.

There isn't money to heat the house. There's oil in the tank, thankfully, but we keep most of the house too cold for comfort, hoping the oil will outlast the winter. Three years ago I built a solar collector that makes 12,000 BTU per hour of heated air on cold, sunny days. It helps a little, and it's 100% free heat. I've worked out plans for two more solar collectors that will together provide another 50,000 or so BTU of free heat. That WILL make a difference, but it's a big project, much more demanding than the first collector was, and I'll be working on the roof.

Through my business account, I've been able to borrow enough money to buy a wood-burning fireplace insert. Seventy-five thousand BTU of heat whether the sun is shining or not, and the only cost is the labor of hauling and splitting wood. I've access to plenty of free firewood.

In case you've been counting BTU, it's a big house. When the children are gone, it will be bigger than Arleen and I need, but the workshops for my business are here, we grow our food on the property, and I haven't the strength to contemplate trying to move everything and start over in a smaller place.

I made some calls to get quotes for having a professional fireplace/chimney specialist install the wood-burning insert. Most said they would not do the installation unless they sold me the flue liner, and I'd already purchased one. The first who said they would be willing was an established company that seemed well qualified, but when I checked with an engineer at the fireplace insert manufacturer, I was told the setup the installer was proposing would not be safe.

I had been thinking I should not try to do the installation myself, but it became clear, I would not get nearly the quality of work from a contractor, no matter how qualified and experienced, as I would be able to accomplish with my own hands under the guidance of the manufacturer's engineers.

Most of the project is straightforward enough, but the flue liner has to be installed from the top of the chimney, more than forty feet above ground. The roof is a twelve/twelve pitch, too steep to stand on. I checked out having a chimney specialist install the flue liner so I could do the rest of the work myself, but the prices were impossibly high. My sense was, nobody really wanted to go up there.

So I spent two or three weeks, pretty much twenty-four seven, puzzling through different scenarios of ladders and ropes, safety harnesses and platforms, trying to work out a way to get on the roof to do the work. And pretty much twenty-four seven of those two or three weeks, I faced the prospect of dying suddenly without getting anywhere close to the top of the chimney.

One of the contractors (who quoted $1,800) said, "That roof, that high, we'll have to stage it." Over the next several days, as I continued to ponder options, I realized he was right. Staging. Steel scaffolding. A forty-foot tower standing on the ground, anchored to the masonry, locked against the house. That would be the only way to do it.

I began to look for scaffolding. I could rent it for $325 a week. One day to go to the supplier, load up and bring it to the house. Another two or three days to set up and tear down. A day to bring it back to the supplier. How much time to actually install the flue liner? And all that while still trying to keep up with my income-producing work. It's doubtful I could finish in one week. In any case if I rented the scaffolding I would be tempted to rush, which is a formula for disaster.

I spent hours on Craigslist looking for used scaffolding. There was some, but nothing suitable. Too many sections, not enough sections, the wrong kind, too much money, too far away... . After several days looking, I thought to search a different word. Instead of "scaffolding," I searched for "staging." Among the listings was a builder who was relocating, selling off material and equipment. I clicked through a dozen or so pictures and came to one that showed the kind of scaffold I needed. I sent an email.

As it happened, he had exactly what I needed. EXACTLY. Exactly the right kind of scaffolding. Exactly the right number of frames. Exactly the right size (e.g., ten-foot cross bracing, not seven). Leveling jacks. Casters. Aluminum planks. Everything.

"How much?"

"Seven hundred dollars."

"I can't afford it. What's your bottom number?"

"I can't go lower than six hundred."

"OK, that's fair. I'll take it."

As it happened, from that day, I had five days left to submit an income statement to the health insurance exchange to avoid losing my coverage. That meant I had to file my federal income taxes before then. It meant I wouldn't be free to pick up the scaffolding for several more days, by which time it might be gone to another buyer. I offered to PayPal the seller $200 to hold it. He declined the deposit and wrote, "I'll hold it for you, Jerry. Just don't let me down."

It was raining lightly when I checked the tires and hooked my faithful, homemade utility trailer to my little diesel Volkswagen. In some traditions a light rain means the gods are pleased with what you are offering, but I worried about hauling my trailer on the Interstate in the rain.

I was tense as I drove, getting a sense of how well the little car with trailer in tow would hold the wet pavement. The car was impressively surefooted, but the trailer tended to fishtail slightly back and forth around curves. I calibrated how much to understeer and how to slow down on straightaways and accelerate gently through curves to minimize the fishtailing. I wondered how it would handle fully loaded. By my calculations, the scaffolding and hardware would max out the carrying capacity of the trailer. I would be pulling 2,000 pounds with my 2,862 pound car. I'd done that before, but it was a long time ago.

The seller, Phil, was about sixty, a few years younger than I. He told me three people wanted to buy the scaffolding after he'd promised it to me. One offered nine hundred dollars. His tone was friendly, with no sign of regret or disappointment. We went about loading 1,200 pounds of steel onto the trailer and securing it for the ride home.

When this was complete, I asked, "What else you got?"

He led me into the building the scaffold had leaned against. The first thing I saw was a wall of small shelves across from where we came in. "Fasteners?" I asked.

"Yeah," he said.

"I could use some lag shields to anchor the staging," I said. "I'll lag into the mortar joints between bricks."

"You don't want lag shields," He said. "You want these." He handed me a box labeled "Hilti Kwik Bolt." It held fifteen or so anchors. "How much?" I asked. "Ten dollars," he said. He went behind a shelf, came back and dropped another dozen or so in the box. "For all of them?" I asked. "Yeah." "Sold," I said. He took some time to explain how to anchor the staging.

"I could use some scrap steel," I told him. "Got any lying around?" "Not really," he said. "I'm not looking for anything in particular. I just need to weld up about eighty pounds for the wedge of this wood splitter I'm working on." I opened the folder I'd brought and showed him what it would look like. "I do have a couple of old snowplow blades," he said. They were perfect, about three-eighths inch thick, four and a half inches wide, nine feet long. "Are you giving them away?" I asked. "Glad to be rid of them," he said.

There were a few more things. Forty feet of rebar to repair my neighbor's hay rake (free). Four and a half feet of steel u-channel hanger strut (free). I didn't know what I might use it for, but that hanger strut would cost thirty dollars at the home center. A Ridgid circular saw in good condition ($25; new they're $100).

The cinder driveway sloped up from where we loaded the trailer. The wheels spun but managed to pull the load up to the main driveway. Again it was uphill before reaching the more level, paved road, a little dead end that served three houses.

The car strained to climb the slope and I wondered if I'd bitten off more than my little four-cylinder VW could chew. I stopped, got out and lay down on the wet pavement beside the trailer. I reached up and felt above the tire to see how much clearance was left before it would rub against the underside of the trailer bed. There was plenty of room, thank God. The springs, which I'd replaced new not many loads ago, had plenty of travel left. They were not overloaded.

As I navigated the local streets toward the Interstate, I discovered, to my relief, the car was not overmatched. And I noticed something else, something quite striking I hadn't expected.

I don't see angels, but I have a strong sense that angels are real and they do see me. From time to time I get clear signals that they care what happens to me. Occasionally I sense their presence, but not always. Now I felt their presence more strongly than I ever had before. The entire drive home, I felt I was being escorted by a hundred, or even hundreds, of divine beings.

I thought a lot about that over the next days. There were other coincidences and clues as well that reinforced my sense of what had happened.

What was that scaffolding for?

The answer: To keep me alive.

Why was the whole episode so synchronistically perfect? The u-channel steel strut, by the way, is exactly what I needed to securely anchor the tower to the woodframe part of the house, at right angles to the side of the chimney I would anchor to with the Kwik Bolts. The length was 54 inches, which when cut yielded three, 18-inch lengths, exactly right to tie into the 2 X 6 wall studs, sixteen inches on center.

The answer: To make it unmistakably clear that none of this was accidental. It was organized intentionally on my behalf.

And to what destination was that host of angels escorting me?

The answer: Back to this life, and I must say, in the days since that drive home, I have felt more alive than I can remember feeling in a very long time.

The woods are lovely, dark and deep
But I have promises to keep
And miles to go before I sleep
And miles to go before I sleep

Epilogue:

I wondered how much the extreme workout had battered my dear little diesel Volkswagen. It turns out, not at all. On the contrary, it runs with noticeably more power than it did before the ordeal (as do I). I had forgotten, that engine thrives pulling loads; it burns the carbon out of the turbocharger so it can breathe like new again. My little horse ...

Mar 12, 2017 2:16pm

Mar 14, 2017 7:46pm

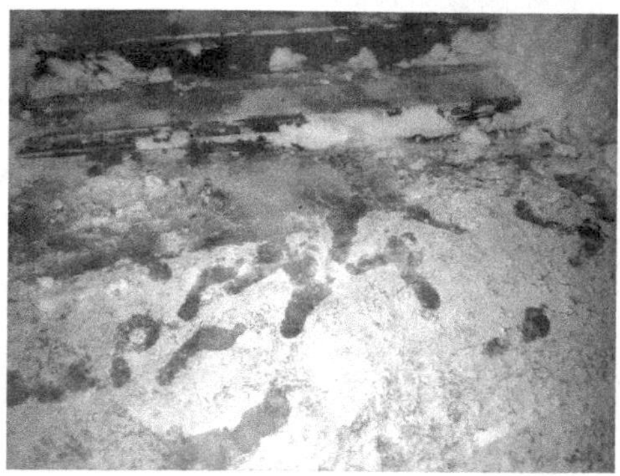

Who needs shoes?

Mar 16, 2017 7:22pm

Mar 16, 2017 8:18pm

"He on whom are woven sky, earth and the space between, also mind, along with all the vital organs — know him alone as one's own Self."

~ *Mundaka Upanishad 2.2.5*

Mar 18, 2017 7:41am

Troubleshooting the dog ...

Lately, Max has been balking at coming down the stairs. So much so, it's been impossible to coax him and I've had to pick him up and carry him, which he tolerates but doesn't like. When we get to the bottom, he wiggles with enthusiasm to go out, forgetting what just happened with the stairs and being carried.

Arleen suggested maybe he's having trouble seeing, so I trimmed his bangs. Boing, boing, boing. Max now goes up and down the stairs happily again.

Mar 18, 2017 7:52am

Christ with me,
Christ before me,
Christ behind me,
Christ in me,
Christ beneath me,
Christ above me,
Christ on my right,
Christ on my left,
Christ when I lie down,
Christ when I sit down,
Christ when I arise,
Christ in the heart of every man who thinks of me,
Christ in the mouth of everyone who speaks of me,
Christ in every eye that sees me,
Christ in every ear that hears me.

~ *Saint Patrick*

O Allah,
place light in my heart,
and on my tongue light,
and in my ears light
and in my sight light,
and above me light,
and below me light,
and to my right light,
and to my left light,
and before me light
and behind me light.

~ *Muslim invocation*

Oh beauty before me,
Beauty behind me,
Beauty to the right of me,
Beauty to the left of me,
Beauty above me
Beauty below me,
I am on the pollen path.

~ *Navaho benediction*

Mar 18, 2017 6:10pm

Today Arleen's been exhausted, irritable and somewhat disoriented.

It seems, unexpectedly and through no intention of her own, she has slipped into an alternate universe and is having trouble functioning in this one. (There's a round-the-clock Downton Abbey extravaganza running on one of her cable stations.)

Mar 20, 2017 2:05pm

Arleen (preparing ingredients for the pot): "Everything has a purpose. Don't touch anything."

Me: "That's an eternal truth, except for the 'don't touch anything' part."

Mar 22, 2017 4:50pm

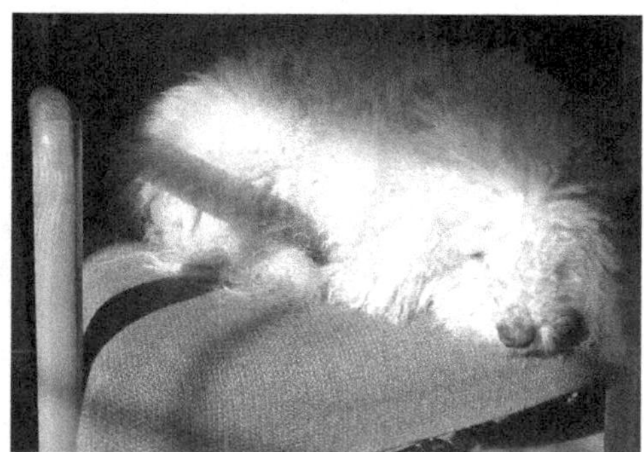

Max found a sunbeam ... in his CHAIR!
Chair AND sunbeam – it's a great day to be a dog

Mar 26, 2017 5:27pm

Wow. Just wow. This morning, pretty much out of the blue, a friend gave me a 1971 South Bend heavy 10 with quite a bit of tooling. FOR FREE. As it sits it's worth about a thousand dollars. After I've done some renovation it will be worth more like three thousand, but I would never sell it. I've wanted exactly that machine for years and years and never been able to get one. Wow.

Mar 29, 2017 9:13am

2:00 am. I moved to turn over in bed and couldn't. My right leg was pinned by something. (Max was using my ankle for a chin rest.)

6:45 am. Children getting ready for school. I can't find the blender jug to make my morning smoothie. "Natasha, have you seen the blender jug?" I ask. "No," she says.

"Max, have you seen the blender jug?" I ask. Then I remembered. In fact, Max had seen it. Last time I was in the kitchen, I put it on the floor for him to clean out. Max is the only one who volunteers to wash dishes.

Mar 30, 2017 11:23am

"Don't come back!" I heard Arleen say as she let Isabella out of the room.

We make bets on how many seconds it will take Isabella to ask to be let back in after she's asked to be let out. Fortunately today there are sunbeams downstairs, so I expect she'll leave Arleen in peace.

Mar 31, 2017 9:26am

"Max," I said, "let's go downstairs and do some yoga." Max didn't wait to go downstairs. As soon as his paws hit the floor, he assumed the downward dog pose and looked up at me expectantly. "This is yoga, right?" he asked.

Mar 31, 2017 6:18pm

Me: "I just gave you one, Max. Remember?"

Max: "Yeah, I remember. That's why I want another one."

Apr 01, 2017 8:38am

Yesterday, I bought five rats (little mother and four babies), which I knew I could get away with because five week old baby rats are the cutest thing in the whole world.

I got them because we've an old rat who has outlived her cage-mates and needs company. Maria talked me into buying two extra babies so she could have her own to take care of. She was so excited to have pet rats of her own again, she cleaned up her room. Miracles will never cease.

Apr 01, 2017 9:10pm

Peanut and Mikey

Apr 04, 2017 12:22pm

"Max," I said, "You take too much of the bed."

"Who, me?"

Apr 05, 2017 8:32pm

Arleen: "It's OK to be good, Maria."

Maria (age sixteen): "No, mom. Shut up."

Apr 07, 2017 4:07pm

Max stood at the bottom of the stairs, conflicted.

Arleen and I were coming down. Maria and Mahlet were going up. We passed each other going up and down.

Max watched carefully and saw, the people coming downstairs didn't have food. He saw, the people going upstairs didn't have food either.

Hmmm ...

There's food in the kitchen, and the kitchen is downstairs.

Max stood pat.

Arleen and I went to the kitchen and Max got to lick some dishes.

Well played, Max.

Apr 07, 2017 5:49pm

The dryer broke down day before yesterday. I took it apart and determined it needed a heating element and drum rollers. I ordered the parts, but they're not here yet. The load of clothes I had put in the dryer when it broke down is still in the laundry room, spread on every available surface to finish drying.

Just now, I went down to the laundry room to bring up a change of clothes. As I was coming up the stairs, I thought of something I wanted to post online. After I'd posted the comment, I looked around and couldn't find the clothes I'd brought up.

"Did I actually bring them up?" I asked myself. I looked around the room again and still didn't see them. Max was in his usual spot, asleep on the bed. Looking closely, I saw that, while I'd been at the keyboard, he had made himself comfortable atop the change of clothes I'd just put there.

Well. Now my change of clothes isn't just dry. It's WARM.

Apr 08, 2017 10:39am

Max sits, gazing worshipfully up at the bowl of breakfast cereal on Maria's night table. Motionless, concentrated, utterly one-pointed. "Max!" I call. He looks at me quickly and then turns back to the object of his devotion. He mutters, "Can't you see I'm busy?"

Apr 08, 2017 12:27pm

Arleen was just visiting in my workroom. All three dogs (Max, Antoine and Isabella) came along. As we talked, she and the dogs played tug-of-war/throw-the-thing with the various plush toys Max has strewn about the room. I kept hearing her say, "Bring it back! Bring it back!" The outcome, I learned, was that, one at a time, Isabella went after each thrown toy, took it downstairs and then came back. Now all the toys are wherever Isabella decided to stash them and there are no plush toys in my workroom.

Apr 09, 2017 12:27pm

Ana (age 20) is visiting.

Max used to sleep in Ana's room, which is now Mahlet's room. Last night, he slept with Ana and Natasha in Natasha's room.

At ten o'clock this morning, I knocked on the door and asked, "Has anyone taken Max out?"

"He just woke up," Natasha called out.

"He ALWAYS just woke up," I said.

Apr 09, 2017 1:51pm

Ana and Max. He'll get his spring shearing soon

Apr 10, 2017 11:52am

Jim came by this morning to drop off two dozen eggs. He's 78, works a little farm with his wife and one or two part-time helpers. Various of our children have worked for Jim and Jasmine over the years. He sat in the cab of his pickup as we chatted, and I noticed he had a black eye.

"What happened?" I asked.

"Well, Saturday night, Jasmine and I were getting ready to go out. She asked, 'How do I look?' and I told her, her panty hose were wrinkled. Turns out, she wasn't wearing panty hose."

Actually, he'd been carrying an armload and tripped over a stone somewhere on his property. No significant damage done, except for the black eye.

Apr 17, 2017 1:20pm

Yesterday I borrowed Jim's tractor and moved the dirt
I'll tidy up with a shovel

The 2X4 braces on the top were to keep the boxes aligned so they don't shift position. When they're all filled with dirt, I'll remove the braces. Ten raised beds, two-and-a-half by five feet.

Whoever built this house never put in a front walk. I'll lay flagstones between the boxes leading to the front door

Apr 17, 2017 7:59pm

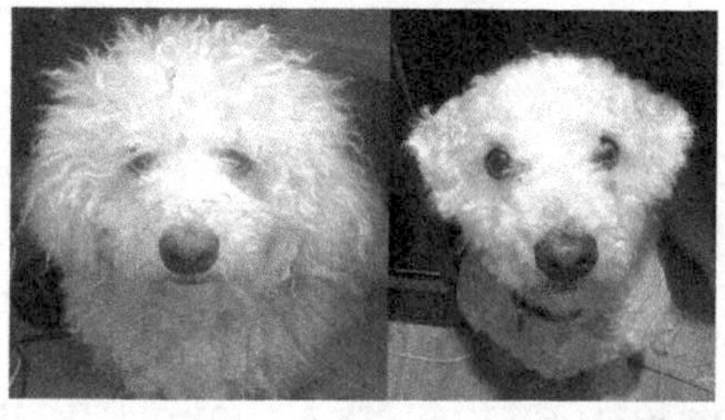

Winter Max/Summer Max (under my desk)

Apr 18, 2017 12:20pm

Winter Max/Summer Max

Apr 19, 2017 10:57am

Ready to plant some vegetables. Taken around 10:30.
In another hour or so, the last three beds will be in the sun

Apr 21, 2017 8:02am

"Max," I said, "you take too much of the bed. We talked about this, remember?"

"No," he said. "Did we?"

Apr 23, 2017 7:29am

"Max," I said, "you're still taking too much of the bed."

"Really? I think YOU'RE taking too much of the bed."

Apr 24, 2017 9:47am

2:00 am, no place to sleep. "Max, I'm moving you over."

He hates being handled when he's been asleep, used to snarl like he would bite your thumbs off. It was like sleeping with a wolf in your bed. He's more cooperative since he's learned he gets a tummy rub if I pick him up in the middle of the night.

"See, there's plenty of room for a dog in this part of the bed."

"Well, the middle's better," he said.

<u>*Apr 24, 2017 8:23pm*</u>

Jim: "If you need the tractor tomorrow, just take it."

Me: "That's the nicest thing anyone ever said to me."

<u>*Apr 25, 2017 6:10pm*</u>

It's not that Max is lazy.

He keeps running back and forth enthusiastically, but he forgets to bring the thing back so I can throw it again. And he keeps looking at me excitedly, like "Something's supposed to happen, right? You're supposed to do something and then I'm supposed to do something, right? Oh, boy this is fun ... what were we doing?"

<u>*Apr 25, 2017 8:57pm*</u>

I stand corrected. Max IS lazy.

"Give him his panda bear," Arleen said.

I looked at Max to see what was going on. It seems, the bear had fallen off the chair and Max didn't want to leave his comfy perch. He looked back and forth at me and Arleen to see which of us he could get to wait on him.

I got up from where I had been sitting and brought Max his bear.

<u>*May 03, 2017 8:24pm*</u>

Max has a parlor game he plays. He comes running into my office and bumps his paws on my leg.

"Hi, Max. 'Sup?"

He looks up toward the top shelf next to my desk. I see his eyes going back and forth between me and where he's pointing his nose.

"Something up there?" I ask.

He licks his chops.

"Something to eat?" I ask.

He starts to wiggle.

"Something to eat UP THERE?" I ask.

He jumps up and down.

"Let me see. Something to eat, up there." I reach up and pull down the bag of dental chew treats. "One of these?" I ask.

"YES, YOU CLUELESS HUMAN!! I MUST HAVE ONE IMMEDIATELY!!!!" he shouts in perfectly clear English.

"Oh! Why didn't you say so?" I ask.

May 06, 2017 12:54pm

"Max," I said, "could you make a little room for the human?" (He's heard these words a hundred times.)

To my surprise, he politely got up and moved over. Then he rolled on his back for a tummy rub.

May 06, 2017 4:20pm

I may have mentioned, Max can count.

He can count to two, which he does like this: "Here's one. Here's another one." That's as high as he can count. After "Here's another one," he loses track. But he can keep track of two.

I often sit at my desk and eat a plate of eggs with a mug of milk. Max, as official dishwasher-in-chief, waits for the dish with some egg yolk to lick off. Sometimes I'll finish the milk without remembering to put the mug down for Max to lick.

"Ahem," he says.

I'll put the mug down, Max cleans it out and then goes over to his napping spot without pestering me for more. He knows, "That was two. I got everything."

Today, as it happens, we're out of milk.

I ate my eggs, put the plate down for Max and went back to what I was doing. After a few minutes, I heard him whimper, and I remembered he'd just finished cleaning the egg plate. "Sorry, Max, we're out of milk. There's only one today." He looked at me incredulously, heaved a sigh and went to lie down.

May 06, 2017 6:28pm

Arleen asked me to find a pot lid. Looking through the cabinets, nothing was where it was supposed to be, which is usually the case.

"There's no logic to how the children put dishes away," I said.

Then I corrected myself. "Actually, there's a perfectly logical logic. They put everything in the closest cabinet until it's full, then they put everything in the next closest cabinet until it's full, and so on until there are no more dishes to put away."

"That's VERY logical," Arleen said.

May 07, 2017 7:26am

1:22 am: Max jumps up suddenly, runs out of the room, up and down the hallway, barking his head off.

3:14 am: Again, Max jumps up suddenly, runs out of the room, up and down the hallway, barking his head off.

"Max! ... Quiet! ... QUIIIEEETTT!!!!" I yell. He stops barking and comes back to bed. "What the hell are you doing?"

"Don't you think it's getting a little monotonous around here?" he asks.

May 12, 2017 9:50pm

"Max," I said, "would you like to go out?"

He jumped up and bounded down the hallway, making a sliding stop at the top of the stairs. He looked back to make sure I was coming and started down the stairs. When he got to the bottom, he made a sharp left turn and headed straight to the kitchen.

"Out is this way, Max."

May 14, 2017 12:05am

Metta Prayer:

May all beings be peaceful.
May all beings be happy.
May all beings be safe.
May all beings awaken to
the light of their true nature.
May all beings be free.

May 14, 2017 8:26pm

Last night, Mahlet went to the senior prom and Natasha and Maria went to a bonfire and sleepover at a friend's house. They all stayed up all night.

In the middle of the afternoon, they were still asleep. Three, THREE humans asleep in their warm, cozy beds in the middle of the day! Needless to say, Max was delighted. It was a good day to be a dog.

May 21, 2017 8:32pm

I ran two tractors and a welding machine today. Life is good.

May 26, 2017 3:30pm

Eight days ago, I ran over some debris that damaged something on my beloved old diesel Volkswagen. From the sound it was making, I was afraid something had happened to the turbocharger (a $1,000+ part). I was afraid to drive it, so I had it towed to the mechanic, who determined I'd damaged the exhaust pipe it was connected to but not the turbocharger itself.

Then Arleen got sick. A very frightening bout of vertigo, from which she's still recovering. Which means she hasn't been able to drive me to pick up my car and likely won't be able to for awhile yet.

So today I asked Jim if there might be a time when he could drive me. "How about now?" he said.

He dropped me off at the mechanic's, I retrieved the keys (I'd already paid over the phone), and I searched the parking lot. When I spotted my seventeen-year-old car in the distance, my eyes teared up and I thought, "That's the most beautiful car I've ever seen."

May 27, 2017 5:32pm

Max sat on Arleen's TV remote and changed the channel. "You didn't like that show?" she asked. "It was a cooking show. I thought you liked cooking shows."

Max looked at Arleen incredulously. He muttered, "What good is a cooking show if you can't SMELL it?"

Jun 02, 2017 6:29pm

Well shoot. Yesterday was Thursday. I had to make a post office run, which meant on the way home I'd be driving past the village recycling transfer station.

I never know what I'll find. This time Dan, the guy who runs the transfer station, had saved some more discarded tomato cages for me. He's been collecting them on my behalf since fall. It looks like I now have enough for this season's planting, which will happen in the next few days.

There was a machine in several pieces on the pavement next to the dumpster. "What's that?" I asked. "It's a wood chipper," Dan said. "It's all there, new blades in the box there. Guy said the only thing wrong is it needs welded where that stud is missing."

"I can fix that," I said. "Can I have it?"

Three hours labor and $3.40 in parts later, I have a good as new Craftsman 8 hp chipper/shredder. Runs like a champ. I'll weld on a tongue so I can tow it around the property with the lawn tractor I rescued from the transfer station a couple of years ago (nothing wrong with it except a blown $8.00 head gasket. It runs like a champ, too!).

Jun 03, 2017 8:13pm

The outcome of Thursday's foraging adventure. Except for the actual hitch coupler, the tongue assembly is welded from found materials. The square steel tubing is a discarded traffic signpost. And of course the wood chipper and the lawn tractor are themselves found items.

Jun 03, 2017 8:17pm

"Note to self ... if at all possible, try not to burn the house down."

That's the thought that passed through my mind as it was occurring to me I'd better remove the gas tank before welding the towing tongue on the wood chipper I've been working on.

Jun 04, 2017 8:46am

Everybody knows that the dice are loaded
Everybody rolls with their fingers crossed
Everybody knows the war is over
Everybody knows the good guys lost
Everybody knows the fight was fixed
The poor stay poor, the rich get rich
That's how it goes
Everybody knows

~ *Leonard Cohen, "Everybody Knows"*

Jun 04, 2017 12:49p

True confession ...
I'm in love with my neighbor's hay rake

It's a New Idea model number 4, which means it's a four-bar hay rake and tedder, manufactured in the late forties or early fifties, near as I can tell. The mechanism is driven by the turning wheels and not by hydraulics or a tractor's power take-off. That means it can be pulled by a horse or mule.

One of the bars broke when Jim was mowing our hayfield last fall. I helped him weld the bar back together (with his stick welder; I hadn't fixed my MIG outfit yet), and the bar broke again.

On closer inspection, the reason the bar broke was, there was damage elsewhere and the bar wasn't properly controlled. I looked it over and told Jim I thought I could fix it.

The first thing to do was, figure out how to get more of the bar material. It was 1-5/16 inches outside diameter. I don't remember what I measured the wall thickness to be, but it turns out the bar was made of schedule 40 steel plumbing pipe. And, as it happens, the bar was 10 feet, 4 inches long. Steel plumbing pipe is made in 21-foot lengths. They had designed the machine around the length of the available pipe to get exactly two bars from each 21-foot length!

Then I had to find a bearing to replace the one that had been lost. There wasn't an exact replacement part available, but it turns out 1-5/16 inch flange bearings are a standard item. It would seem, lots of people use schedule 40 steel plumbing pipe to build machinery. With my newly restored MIG welder, I welded up some steel to replace the destroyed mounting surface and worked out the fit.

I drilled the new bar for the tines to bolt on and looked for new tines and new tine clamps to replace the missing ones. Tines I was able to find, but the clamps weren't available anywhere. So I figured out how to fashion them. That involved welding up a nice anvil, which I'll post pictures of when I have them.

The renovation is almost done.

Jun 05, 2017 7:24pm

Synchronicity ...

As I sat at my desk, behind me I heard skittering claws on the hardwood floor. Back and forth, round and round, lots of excited skittering. I turned around and found Max, all wound up, boingboingboing, with a wild look in his eye.

"What is it, Max?" I asked.

He bounded toward the door, looking back to see if I was following, so excited he couldn't stop and wait for me. He bounded up and back along the hallway ahead of me as I walked, impatient for me to arrive where he wanted me to go.

Sometimes it's a little tricky figuring out where a dog wants to take you if there are distractions along the way. Maria's door is halfway down the hall, and she almost always has food in her room. Max paused at her doorway, but then continued on toward the stairs.

He paused again at the top of the stairs. They're still a bit of a puzzle for Max, whose short legs and long body aren't well adapted for such terrain. I have to go ahead of him and then encourage him to follow, which I did and he did.

As I got to the bottom of the stairs, I expected to find a freshly baked casserole or plate of cookies on the kitchen island. When Max acts like that, it's usually because there's something exciting in the kitchen and he wants to visit it.

And, in fact, there was something very interesting on the kitchen island. A jar of pickles. Next to it was a note, in urgent red marker: "Open please!"

There was nothing else. I've no idea what Max was so excited about, but I opened the jar, came upstairs and reported the event to Arleen.

Jun 09, 2017 5:21pm

The repair on Jim's hay rake is complete
Now I have to finish making some replacement clamps
to attach the missing tines

Jun 10, 2017 8:31pm

The hay rake project has driven some big improvements in my shop setup:

1. When I started the project, I didn't have a working welder. I had been intimidated by the prospect of tearing down my broken MIG welder and replacing the failed diode. When I opened the welder, I found it wasn't complicated at all. Now, after ten years' downtime, it welds like new again.

2. I needed an anvil to fashion sixteen replacement tine clamps for the rake. VERY useful to have a nice little anvil (on wheels!) in my workshop.

3. To weld the hay rake, I needed a way to get the welder down to the rake. I didn't want to improvise something awkward that would multiply the effort, so I designed and fabricated a welding cart. For the chassis, I reconfigured a power washer cart I salvaged from the recycling transfer station.

The top of the push handle on the donor cart was narrower than I needed, so I cut it apart and welded more tubing to match the width of the finished welding cart.

I shortened the axle so the wheels would fit underneath and not stick out the sides. That way, it will go through narrower spaces without hanging up. On the opposite end from the picture, under the coiled cables, is a little drawer at the bottom. Welding wire, MIG gun tips, etc. go in there. There are two wooden boxes behind the shielding gas bottle (only the top one is showing). They are interchangeable and removable. Pretty much all the needed tools and accessories fit.

The welding cart is made 100% from found materials. The 1-1/4 inch angle iron is old bed frames, along with some ¾-inch angle iron I found behind Jim's barn. The donor cart had two flat tires when I brought it home. I pulled out the inner tubes and found no leaks. I pumped them up and they've held air ever since.

This was a great apprentice welding project, and my skill has improved as a result. While Arleen watches her cooking shows in the other room, I've been watching YouTube videos on how to weld auto-body repairs. When I can get to it, I'll cut out the rusted rocker panel and some smaller rusted areas on her Grand Caravan and weld in new metal.

Jun 11, 2017 12:24pm

Today, like yesterday, will be hot and dry. First thing, I went around to see how the various plantings looked from last night's watering. I thought, "I might want to run a hose out to where I planted sunflower seeds by the road." It's farther than a 100-foot hose will reach, but I have some shorter sections I can piece together.

When I went out to see how my sunflower seedlings are doing, I saw that my neighbor Jim had destroyed half of them with his tractor when he was mowing yesterday to get mulch for his farm. I couldn't understand how he did that, as I'd talked to him often about the planting. I'd used his tiller to prepare the plot. It was clearly a planting bed, full of seedlings on tilled earth, unmistakably different from the turf next to it. But he drove his tractor right over half of it.

I called him and gently told him I was upset about what he'd done. He apologized, and I said, "Thank you."

Jim is the one person in the world I would choose to be in a dispute or misunderstanding with. He is the fairest person I have ever known, with no trace of defensiveness or meanness. If something's wrong, you just tell him. He asks a few questions if need be. He explains what happened from his point of view if need be. And the matter dissolves, always leaving a clearer connection than before the conflict.

Jim is 78 years old, and I dread the day he's gone. As far as I know, he's in excellent health. He's stronger than I am. May he live to be a hundred and twenty.

I dropped Mahlet off at her job at the Eastbrook Mall, still feeling crushed over what had happened to my sunflowers. I had planned to drive on to Wal-Mart and pick up some spray paint to match the green of the hay rake. It would only take a few minutes to paint the repairs, and it's the kind of thing I enjoy doing.

As I turned into the entry road for Wal-Mart, I saw a man standing on the sidewalk. I'd seen him several times before, typically a week or two of absence between. He looks in his fifties, I would say, with sandy whiskers flecked with white. Beaten down. Shoulders slumped, gaze downward, standing motionless in the bitter cold or blazing sun, always with the same, ragged little corrugated cardboard sign: "Homeless veteran."

I calculated my finances and figured I could give him ten dollars. I give him a twenty when I can, but this week is pretty thin. I haven't gotten enough work done since Arleen's bout of vertigo two weeks ago. She said it was worse than her open heart surgery. She's still dizzy but a little better every day. Two days ago she rode in a car for the first time since the onset, and now she's been able to get outside and water her planter boxes and raised beds again. That gives her pleasure.

There won't be money to pay the mortgage on time. I think I can scrape enough to get it paid by the end of the month, but there will be a $95 penalty. Not a big deal in the grand scheme of things. My homeless veteran is standing on the sidewalk begging. I've no idea where he sleeps.

I found my paint and picked out two bananas to eat in the car. Went through the checkout and forgot to get ten dollars cash back. "I'll get another banana," I thought. But as I went through the line again, I thought, "I really only want two bananas. Oh yeah, of course. The third one is for my homeless friend. Forgetting the ten dollars wasn't really an accident, I guess."

I pulled over to the sidewalk and held out the banana through the passenger side window. "Here's something for you," I said. "And here's something to keep you going," I added, handing him the ten.

I straightened from leaning over to reach out the window and drew my hand back. He reached into the car and took my hand in his. "God bless you," he said in a gentle voice, "God bless you." His voice seemed angelic in its sweetness. "God bless you, my friend," I said and drove away, tears in my eyes, as is the case every time I encounter that man.

Jun 13, 2017 1:38pm

I believe that unarmed truth and unconditional love will have the final word.

~ Martin Luther King, Jr.

Jun 13, 2017 7:00pm

My work here is done

That's me in the first picture, Jim in the second. When he's finished bolting on the new tines, that venerable machine will be ready for the season's first haying.

In the third picture, you see two new tines installed. The one on the left is attached with an old tine clamp. Sixteen clamps were missing so I fashioned replacements from scrap metal, as you see on the right.

Jun 13, 2017 7:44pm

"Before you can do anything, you always have to do something else first."

~ Murphy's Law: Section 2, Paragraph VI

Here's the anvil I built to fashion replacement tine clamps for Jim's hay rake.

Note the Art Deco style of the wooden base (e.g., the Empire State Building; Jim wants to paint little windows on it). This developed organically.

The three outriggers at the bottom create a tripod structure that won't rock. They serve as feet, protruding 1/4 inch below the rest of the base so the middle of the base doesn't touch the ground.

The wheels also don't touch the ground until you tip the anvil back, using the horn as the steering handle. It rolls nicely. Agile, easy to move around.

The wood is entirely glued. The only metal fasteners are long screws into the four by four outriggers to prevent them from splitting. It's made entirely from found materials except for the striking surface, which is a four-by-six-inch, hardened-steel jeweler's anvil block I purchased online for $20.

The anvil is mounted to the wooden base with lag screws and seated in a bed of epoxy to create a monolithic connection. It transmits hammer force to the workpiece beautifully and is fairly quiet to use, doesn't ring loudly because the monolithic structure lowers the resonant frequency and dampens the higher frequency sound waves.

The lower step of the top surface is mild steel from scrap I had on hand. I discovered you can create a custom shaping form for a special task, weld it to the mild steel and pound the workpiece to the desired shape. Then when you're done, you can cut off the welds and go to the next project.

What you see welded to that surface now is the setup for forging the tine clamps. I've welded the stirrup of an old tine to a section of the original bar it was mounted to, and I've added some heavy angle to make a flat surface under the legs of the tines so I could hammer the metal being formed.

The last picture shows examples of the tine clamps, old and new (forged on that anvil), front and back. On the bottom left of that picture, you see my left foot. It may interest you to know if you mow grass barefooted, your feet turn green.

Jun 13, 2017 9:24pm

Quote of the day: "That's the ugliest, most functional anvil I've ever seen."

Jun 16, 2017 3:11pm

Visitors in my garden

Found this nest in an untended corner of the garden enclosure. Notice anything? (There's a cowbird egg in with the three song sparrow eggs.)

Jun 16, 2017 6:00pm

Max wants everyone to know, there's a pizza on the kitchen island and he can't reach it. This is an urgent situation.

Jun 17, 2017 7:56am

I've fallen in love with a bird ...

Checked on mama song sparrow this morning. When I went out on the deck, I saw her fly up from her nest, which means she's continuing to sit on her eggs after I removed the cowbird's egg. She flew up and perched atop one of the garden enclosure posts. Dowdy-looking little ball of nondescript brown-speckled fluff. She preened herself as I watched through my binoculars. Adorable.

According to what I've read, small songbirds sit on their eggs about 50% of the time during incubation, so I needn't worry if sometimes she isn't there.

Now I have to rethink how I'm going to work the garden enclosure. I'll leave the weeds alone around the area where she's nesting, I guess, and arrange the plantings differently than I'd planned. There's plenty of room.

The raised beds are done, but I haven't planted my seedlings in the main garden yet. I was getting ready to do that when I discovered the nest.

Jun 19, 2017 11:14am

Discouraged.

Very tired. Not enough money to pay for food and medicine. Buried in high interest consumer debt I can't refinance because my debt to income ratio is too high even though my FICO score is over 700, so I pay $400 - $600 per month in interest. This was debt I accumulated over a decade or more trying to keep the household together for the children.

The problem isn't a lack of orders. When I get tired, my production slows down, and with it my income. I've been overtaxed taking care of all the household driving, etc., while Arleen's recovering from her bout of vertigo. She's been sick three weeks. She's much better and continuing to improve daily, but she's still dizzy and can't drive.

Jun 20, 2017 7:26pm

Dogs can tell time. Did you know that?

Max comes into my room, all excited. "It's time for my treat!" he says.

"Oh, is that so?" I ask.

"Yeah," he said. "I want a treat, so that's what time it is."

Jun 21, 2017 4:20pm

Mama song sparrow's babies have hatched. There probably won't be pictures soon, however. She's gotten used to me and lets me get within a couple of feet before she hops down from her nest, but I don't want to bother her too often.

Jun 24, 2017 7:57pm

Rocks rolling around in my head.

(Google "benign paroxysmal positional vertigo." Gotta find a doctor who's good at parking otoliths.)

Jun 25, 2017 6:36pm

Two humans and a dog had the gall to walk down the street in front of our house.

Max was deeply offended.

Jun 26, 2017 10:01pm

The dizzy spells have stopped. Repeated the Epley maneuver this evening. No spinning, no nystagmus. Some guidelines say continue the maneuver for a week. I'm undecided at this stage. Feeling pretty much back to normal.

Jun 27, 2017 2:08pm

Mahlet wears dark lipstick, and she adores Max

Jun 27, 2017 9:03pm

Dog logic.

Max is sitting here while I work on a batch of fifty whistleheads. I have an episode of American Ninja Warrior running on my computer to keep the boredom in check. Lots of cheering, sudden noises, loud announcer. Not a peep out of Max. Break to commercial. There's a teaser for The Tonight Show. In one of the bits, Jimmy Fallon says something after inhaling helium. Max barks.

Jun 28, 2017 8:29am

Holy shit! Bicycles!!! Max is barking his head off. How dare they ride bicycles on our street!

Jun 28, 2017 1:23pm

It gets worse and worse. Now Jim's tractor is here mowing the hayfield.

Jun 29, 2017 8:26am

Every year, a nestful of adolescent barn swallows spend a week or two topping off their body weight and learning to forage for themselves by lining up on the rain gutter over our deck while Mom and Dad circle and dart over the hayfield and come zooming back to stuff a bug in one or another of the kid's mouths.

How's that for a long sentence!

I hadn't seen them and wondered if they would show up this year. Yesterday, after Jim mowed the hay and created a bonanza for the barn swallows, I saw three of them lined up on the gutter. Last year there were five. These three are likely the children of some of those, or perhaps the next brood of their siblings.

Jun 29, 2017 12:35pm

Genia, who is at college in Binghamton, New York, drove down to bring back Natasha, who has been visiting her. Along for the visit came Genia's boyfriend, Adam, and Genia's girlfriend's five-year-old son, Mchale, whom Genia and Adam are babysitting.

Last night, Max slept with Genia and Adam. And he slept with Mchale. And he slept with Maria. And he slept with me. It's a great day to be a (snuggly) dog.

Jun 29, 2017 7:07pm

"In love all the contradictions of existence merge themselves ... and are lost. Only in love are unity and duality not at variance. Love must be one and two at the same time."

~ *Rabindranath Tagore*

Jun 29, 2017 7:51pm

The barn swallow kids, class of '17, waiting for supper

Jun 30, 2017 2:12pm

Behold, the hay rake!

Jun 30, 2017 4:39pm

Baling the hay

Jun 30, 2017 4:40pm

Max had a bath. Now he's blissfully wriggling himself dry on my bedding.

Jun 30, 2017 4:43pm

Take one dog, add water

Jul 01, 2017 9:35am

The baby song sparrows have left the nest. According to an online source:

"As early as the age of seven days, nestlings can often survive if they fall from their nest. The maximum time stayed in the nest is about fourteen days. Once on the ground, the young birds continue to be fed by their parents until the age of 28 to 80 days; during this time they are referred to as fledglings."

I didn't see any birds this morning, but they're very small and I expect they're well hidden in the undergrowth. Now I'm faced with a dilemma. They're inside the garden enclosure, most of which is surrounded by seven-foot-tall deer netting, which can ensnare young birds. I think I'll have to take down the netting.

Note: I didn't take the deer netting down and no birds got stuck.

Jul 02, 2017 8:00pm

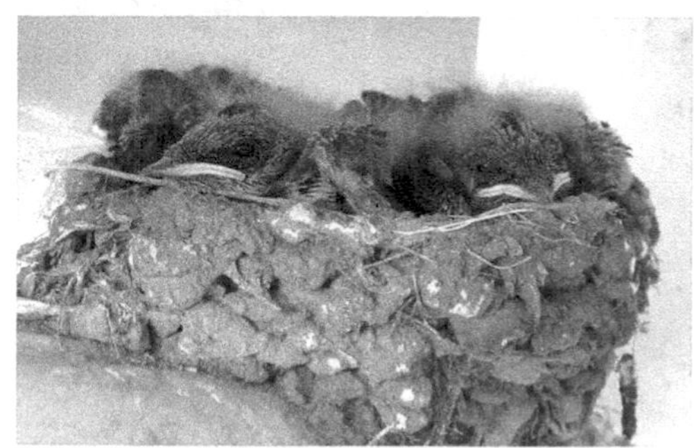

The barn swallow kids, class of '17 and-a-half

Jul 02, 2017 8:08pm

The wild blackberries are ripe. This evening, I feasted on the big blackberry thicket on the north side of the house. I've been cultivating that thicket for several years, and it's thriving.

As I began to pick berries, I heard, "Meow!"

"Momma catbird?" I called. "Is that you?"

"Meow! Meow!"

I talked to her as I picked berries, eating as fast as I could pick them. From the middle of the blackberry thicket, her calls became more insistent. But she didn't fly away, even though I was only three feet from her perch.

"MEOW!! MEOW!!!! MEOW!!!!"

She scolded me for a long time and then became quiet. I didn't hear rustling leaves or flapping wings, so I think she just waited for me to finish foraging her blackberry thicket and go away.

HER blackberry thicket. Make no mistake.

Jul 03, 2017 8:33pm

At the grocery store today, I noticed the cashier, a young woman, had a large tattoo on her forearm. I asked if I could see it. She seemed pleased as she held it up for me to view. It was a traditional Japanese form, a koi (large goldfish), beautifully rendered.

The tattoo seemed spare, however, and I realized that was because the only color was black. "Are you going to get some color done to it?" I asked. "Yeah," she said. "When I get some money saved."

"It's a beautiful tattoo," I said as I finished my purchase. "Thank you," she said, smiling brightly. "Have a nice day!"

There was something else about the tattoo I noticed, but I wasn't sure what it was. Then in the parking lot it struck me. Her forearm was streaked with long, whitish lines, the marks of self-harming, perhaps suicide attempts. The tattoo would cover them, eventually.

I wondered if I could have said anything more to let her know I understand something of what she'd been through (I attempted suicide twice myself as a teenager), and especially, that there are people who care about her, even people she's never met.

Finally, I concluded I had conveyed the message well enough. I care about her, and she could tell.

Jul 04, 2017 8:56pm

Arleen told me she found a dying bird in front of the house. She said it was on the ground, eyes open, quivering. She petted it and wished it well. Then she came back inside to tell me.

"Where?" I asked.

"Beside the hose reel, by the raised beds."

That would be directly under the nest of baby barn swallows.

"Show me," I said.

We went out and she showed me the spot, but there was no bird. I searched the underbrush. Still no bird. "I think it must have flown against the house and was just stunned," I said. "It must have recovered and flown off."

In the next half hour, I was thinking, "What if that bird got away from there, but died somewhere else? That was likely the mother of the babies in the nest. Is there still an adult bird to feed them?"

I saw no barn swallows in the air, so I hatched a plan. Barn swallows always appear when you start a lawn mower. They actually respond to the sound of the motor, I've observed. I would do some mowing near the nest to stir up bugs for them to catch and see if the parents showed up.

After I'd run the mower back and forth awhile, I still saw no barn swallows.

"OK," I thought. "I'll get the stepladder and climb up close to the nest like I did when I took the picture. Momma barn swallow swooped close and scolded me then. That might get her to make an appearance if she's OK."

I went to the garage to get the ladder. As I carried it toward the nest, I saw a barn swallow darting nearby. "OK," I thought. "Now is that barn swallow connected with those babies?" There are lots of barn swallows here. We see eight or ten at a time. "I want to see her feed the chicks."

I put the ladder back in the garage and came back out. Sat on the front porch and watched. There were two barn swallows zooming over the front yard. Good sign, might be both parents.

Then I saw it. One of them flew to the nest, paused a split second, and flew back up in the air to catch more bugs. "Great," I thought. "They're getting fed."

Carry on, Momma barn swallow.

Jul 08, 2017 2:11pm

I was weeding in the garden when Mahlet, age 17, came to bring the car key.

"I hate nature!" She said.

"What happened?" I asked.

"I'm being attacked!"

"By what?"

"Ladybug!" she said. "They're vicious."

Right.

Jul 09, 2017 8:36pm

Three (or was it four) years ago at the Pipers' Gathering, I had a brainstorm. In a few hours time, I designed a machine to polish brass whistle tonebodies much more efficiently than the way I'd been doing it on my machinist lathe. It took three (or was it four) years, off and on, to complete the machine and get it working as intended. Today, it is done ...

The 1" X 30" belt sander is on a hinge that lowers it horizontal to press down on the brass tube.

To the right and left of the polishing belt you see four wheels. I made them from rollerblade wheels, cut down on the lathe to the diameter I needed. Behind them, you see two springs against which the roller assembly moves up and down. The springs provide the pressure for the wheels to push down on the brass tube and hold it in the long roller carriage underneath.

In front of the belt sander assembly you see the two long rollers that position the brass tube under the polishing belt. Both rollers are clad with latex tubing to grip the brass.

One of the rollers of the carriage is driven by the motor to the right of the machine. I reduced the diameter of the motor shaft to adjust the speed of the driven roller. It's connected by a vacuum cleaner belt and spins the brass tube the opposite direction of the polishing belt. Above the long rollers are three small bearings that form a backstop to keep the brass tube from spinning off the rollers.

To the left of the belt sander you see a long wand, the end of which fits into the end of a tonebody tube so I can push it through the machine. The end of the wand that fits into the tonebody has bearings inside so it can spin along with the tonebody as it is spinning under the buffing belt.

And to the left of that you see a few tubes that have been polished.

Jul 12, 2017 10:32am

Max loves Maria. When she's home, he spends most of his time with her. This morning, I found him hanging out at my end of the hallway.

"What's up, Max?" I asked. He got up from where he was lying and led me to Maria's door. I knocked. Maria, barely awake, said, "What?" I opened the door and let Max into Maria's room.

I expected him to jump up on her bed, his favorite place in the house. But he ignored Maria completely and headed straight to the peanut butter and jelly sandwich on her bedside table.

On second thought, Maria's bed is Max's second favorite place in the house. His favorite place is the kitchen.

Jul 12, 2017 4:15pm

Max is busy. In case anyone wants him, they'll have to wait. He's watching Natasha eat a deviled egg sandwich.

Jul 12, 2017 4:24pm

I'm having some success teaching Max not to bark so much. Max, on the other hand, is having less success training his human to provide treats on command. The human, it seems, keeps moving the goal posts.

The original deal was, if Max barked for a legitimate reason and then stopped barking on my command, he got a treat. For awhile, he tried barking for no reason at all and then stopping, but that didn't get treats. (Stupid human.)

The last time I gave him a barking-related treat, though, he didn't bark at all. There was some kind of commotion outside and he really, REALLY wanted to bark, but he didn't. Instead, he made dog throat-clearing noises. "Ahem. Ahem, there! I'm too polite to bark, but I think you should know, there's something going on out there." Of course, he got a treat immediately.

Today, he barked at a thunderclap. I told him to be quiet, and he stopped barking, came over, wagged his tail, licked his chops and eagerly looked up at the shelf with the bag of treats. I had to think that one through. If I gave him a treat, would he bark less or more? I decided not to give him a treat.

"Sorry, Max. Nice try."

"Stupid human."

Jul 16, 2017 3:22pm

An adventure in paradise ...

My musical friends will know, Catskills Irish Arts Week concluded last night. Always a magical time, not to be missed.

A week or so ahead of the event, I was still feeling wobbly after a hellish bout of benign paroxysmal positional vertigo a couple of weeks previous. The nauseating, wild, room-spinning vertigo had resolved after Arleen and I performed the Dix Hallpike test and then the Epley maneuver to get the runaway otolith crystals parked where they wouldn't roll around in one of the inner ear's semicircular canals. But I've continued to have some slight dizziness, and I've felt a bit fragile ever since.

So I decided not to go.

Circumstances, however, did not cooperate. I realized I had no choice but to attend, as I wouldn't make it through the month without the income from my vendor's table. (I've found I only need to attend the last three days; I do exactly the same business in three days as I do if I come for the full week.)

So I called to book a room at Weldon House, where I always stay, only to discover it was full, as was the Blackthorn Lodge, which runs both facilities. So I called Gavin's Irish Country Resort and was told there was a cancellation and one room had become available. The price included meals in the restaurant, which I wouldn't need (I bring my own food), and it was more than I was used to paying, but I was pretty sure it was the only room left in all of East Durham, so I made the reservation.

I had a mountain of work to complete before I could go, and somewhat limited energy, but I've done enough of these events now, I can gauge pretty well how to get everything ready without burning out too badly. I did in fact finish the last of the preparations within minutes of when I needed to hit the road if I were to get there in time to set up for the evening's concert.

The car was oven-hot from the sun. I opened all four doors so it could air out while I finished packing (the air conditioning has never worked). Half an hour later, when I brought my stuff to the driveway, it was pouring rain. I'd already loaded a banker's box full of food and personal effects on the passenger seat. The corrugated box was soaked and nearly melted. No time to exchange it, though, so I hoped it would air dry during the drive.

It didn't. The cardboard was too weakened to support the contents, so I would have to find another box when I got to the inn.

The drive was tedious, with slowdowns due to road construction, but otherwise uneventful. The GPS said it would take two and a half hours, but it took three. My spirits lifted as I rolled into East Durham, where the magical atmosphere of Irish Arts Week filled the street.

I heard a familiar "clunk" sound in the back of my car and thought, "What's up with that?" Glancing at the dashboard, I saw the "trunk open" symbol was lit. "Nuts," I thought. "How did that happen?" I pulled over, got out and closed the trunk. Within seconds of driving away, I heard, "clunk." I stopped again and closed the trunk again. And again, as soon as I was moving, "clunk."

So I drove on to Gavin's, hoping the trunk lid would stay down and nothing would fall out.

I checked in and asked the person at the desk where I might find a cardboard box. "I'll call the pantry," she said. She picked up a phone and I heard her ask, "Do you have any boxes?" She pointed me in the direction and said, "It's the screen door."

I went to the screen door and called, "Hello!" Someone came to the door and pointed left. "Dining room's over there," he said and hurried away. I called again, "Hello, I need ... " Another person called from inside, "Other door!" Finally I got someone to pay attention. "I need a box. You people keep trying to get rid of me." "Sorry," he said. "Here are some boxes. Do you see any you can use?" I found a suitable box and went back to my car.

As I drove around to my parking spot, I wondered, "Why is the trunk latch opening?" Rainwater in the switch, I figured out, from leaving the door open in the downpour. So I closed the windows, put the car heater temperature to the hottest setting and turned the fan up all the way. I left it like that for the rest of the night's driving, and by the time I returned to my room after the concert, the problem had stopped.

I don't wear shoes if I can possibly avoid it. I'd brought a good pair of flip-flop sandals, the ones I'd worn with a sport coat and polo shirt at the Science and Nonduality Conference last October. At events, the sandals stay parked under my vendor's table and I'm barefoot. "Like Tolstoy," someone commented.

I rolled up to the pavilion where Thursday evening's concert would begin in an hour's time. As I stepped out of the car, I sensed something was amiss with my left foot. Looking down, I saw the webbing had broken and the thong had come away from the sole of my sandal. I couldn't walk with it, so I took off both sandals and went to work.

Later, when there was some slack time at the table, I worked out a repair that could be done with the tools and materials I had on hand. It was a little uncomfortable, but a strong repair and it looked OK. The rest of the evening was routine, not a lot of business, but that was normal for the first night. Friday night and the all-day Saturday concert are always the busy times.

I drove back to my room, exhausted, and fell into bed. I awoke feeling renewed, but very hungry, and truth be told, lonely. I live what feels like a sort of exile's life. It's just my own psychological makeup and nothing "real," but I've always felt like a sort of outsider guest in several communities, with none that quite feels like "home" (Irish music, Transcendental Meditation, nondual spirituality, Christianity, Judaism, the town where I grew up, etc.).

Feeling adrift, I walked over to the dining area and saw a buffet breakfast was arranged outside, with picnic tables under a canopy. Only three people were seated, so I filled my plate and joined them. Two men, maybe in their fifties, and a young man, maybe late teens or early twenties, with flaming red hair. "He looks like a young Sean Smyth," I thought.

I ate silently while the men talked about a friend's business project. I couldn't tell exactly what. It sounded like the friend had invented something and was working out how to market it. Eventually, one of the men turned to me and asked, "Are you enjoying the week?" "I just got here last night," I said. "I'm a vendor. I make whistles."

"You're Jerry Freeman!" He said. "I have several of your whistles. I love them." All three men enthusiastically talked whistles, and I began to feel a little less lost. The topic came around to Clarke "originals," the conical, rolled and soldered tinplate whistles with the wooden fipple block. "It's a sound that's been lost to the music," I said, "because they're not very good from the factory. People don't know how to tweak them, so nobody plays them. It's a terrific whistle when it's been set up well."

The young man was keenly interested, so with pen and napkin, I drew for him the details of how to turn a Clarke original into a world-class Irish whistle. Someday, I'll manufacture them myself. That voicing needs to come back to the music.

As I got up to leave the table, one of the men said, "Thank you. Thank you for your generosity."

(This happens again and again, by the way, whether it's music events or meditation meetings or mowing hay. I forget that people care about me and appreciate what I have to offer. Someday, maybe, I'll get it through my head and not have to be reminded every time.)

On the way up the stairs to my room, I felt something go amiss with my right foot.

"No," I thought. "It couldn't be." I looked at my sandal and sure enough, it had broken exactly the same way the left one had the night before. "I've had these sandals five years," I thought. "What are the odds they would both break within twelve hours of each other."

I put the sandals aside and set up to work on whistles, preparing for the evening's business at the concert. As I worked, I thought about the broken sandal and decided to stop and repair it. But I couldn't find the piece that anchored the webbing to the sole, so I couldn't fix it.

I got in the car and drove into East Durham to look for flip-flops.

I went into Lawyer's General Store, looked around and found a rack of flip-flops and water shoes. Women's and children's sizes only (except for the water shoes, which weren't what I wanted). There were none that would fit. So I drove down the block to East Durham Hardware. "Do you have flip-flops?" I asked. "Over here," the man said.

For $2.99, I found the cheapest looking grey flip-flops you could imagine, and the only size I could wear was about two sizes too big. But I needed flip-flops, and I knew there wasn't another pair to be purchased in East Durham, so I bought them. "Will you guarantee these will last two days?" I asked the store manager. "No," he said, and we both laughed.

Trying them out, I found they were dangerous to wear. The soles stuck out so far in front and back, they would catch on things as I walked and trip me up. Not to mention, they looked like clown shoes. I wondered if I could trim them to size. The only scissors I'd brought were a small pair of barber shears I use for some of the fine cutting I have to do. But sure enough, it cut through the soft foam soles, and the finished product looked respectable. Finally I had a pair of sandals I could wear safely, without embarrassment.

I finished the afternoon's whistle preparations, loaded the car and got ready to drive to the pavilion to set up for the evening.

When I turned the key in the ignition, the car alarm went off. "Nuts," I thought. "What's that about?" I turned the engine off and on again. The alarm continued. HONK! HONK! HONK! HONK! ... I got out and locked and unlocked the doors from outside. The alarm continued. I got back in and started the car. The alarm continued. Eventually, the alarm stopped by itself for no apparent reason and I drove to the pavilion. I parked the car and took the key out of the ignition. The alarm went off again. HONK! HONK! HONK! HONK! ... People looked at me. "My car is trying to embarrass me!" I called to them. They stopped looking. Finally the honking stopped and I unloaded.

The evening went well. A good amount of business, a lot of friendly conversation, many people telling me how much they appreciate my work. And wonderful music, with a lot of poignant, mournful singing about leaving home and family, love and loss, old age and dying. Several times that night, I fought tears.

The thing is, I'm getting old.

I can't do some things I used to, and lately I've been wondering, with the dizziness, will I be able to mount forty feet of scaffold and do the chimney work for the new wood-burning fireplace insert so we can keep the house warm enough this winter? I've been feeling doubtful and diminished, not sure how I'll be able to carry on.

After the concert, I loaded my boxes and started the car. HONK! HONK! HONK! HONK! ... . As I drove off, I shouted to the onlookers, "I'm stealing my own car!" There was nothing more to be done about it that night. In the morning, when the inn lobby was open again, I could use the public computer to go online and search "2000 VW Jetta how to turn off alarm."

After breakfast, I went online and found the instructions I needed. Disconnect the positive battery cable. Turn the ignition key ten times on and off. Turn it on again and hold it five to ten seconds. You should hear a click. Reconnect battery cable.

I got a wrench out of the trunk and followed the instructions. I was doubtful of the key-turning business. It seemed, with the battery disconnected, nothing was happening. I turned the key the final time and held it ten seconds. No click.

"OK," I thought. "I wonder if that did anything."

I reconnected the battery and started the car. Silence, except for the sweet sound of my little horse's diesel engine. "Is it really fixed?" I thought. (Yes, it was really fixed. I think probably, the key-turning routine was bogus. Likely just disconnecting and reconnecting the battery was enough to reset the alarm.)

I finished the morning's preparations and drove to the pavilion, arriving a little after 11:00 for the event scheduled to begin at noon. Within the first half-hour, my table was very busy and I hurried to keep enough whistles ready on the table. A man about my own age came over and held out a battle-worn pre-1980's key of D redtop brass Generation. "I've played this for years and years," he said. "I bought it in 1970. It doesn't work like it used to."

The windway roof was completely worn off the first quarter inch of the beak, leaving the inside of the windway exposed. The windway floor was severely warped in an arch, closing off about half the original opening at the downwind end. And the inside of the mouthpiece was covered with a layer of crust from hundreds, maybe even thousands of hours of playing.

"Let me see what I can do," I said.

I love those old, classic Generation whistles. Generation replaced the tooling in the early 1980's and the whistles have never been the same. The really good vintage ones are special and it delights me to bring them back to life, which I get to do two or three times a year.

A few months ago, I stopped offering tweaked Generations in Eb, D and C. As they come from the factory the whistles no longer can be reliably tweaked, so I had to give up on them. (High G, F, Bb, alto A and tenor G tweaked Generations, however, are turning out better than ever.) Pondering the implications, I understood what to do.

When the University of Connecticut provided me with CT scans of my whistle designs, I also got scans of good examples of pre-1980's Generation Eb/D, C and Bb whistleheads. I will turn those scans into 3D printing designs and create replicas of the original, treasured Generation whistles. It will take some time, as the technology and materials are still evolving, but I will do it, I promise. Those classic whistles MUST come back.

The 1970 redtop brass Generation was in rough shape. There was nothing I could do to repair the damaged windway roof, and I wouldn't try to change the distorted interior geometry. This is archival work, and I take a very light touch to the original plastic on these historic instruments. I could do two things:

1. Meticulously clean the whistle. I removed the crust from inside so not a single particle could be seen when sighting through the windway. Very important not to leave even the smallest crumb, as it will disturb the airstream and damage the sound.

2. I installed a filler lattice under the windway. People stick a ball of poster putty to fill the cavity under the windway, and that cleans up some of the unstable notes. But poster putty or any solid filler deadens the sound. It took me ten years to finally come up with a solution I was satisfied with. I needed something transparent to sound waves, but that an airstream would see as a solid surface. Finally, I figured out how to create an open lattice that attaches under the windway. It works perfectly without altering the original plastic in any way.

I finished that work and tried the whistle. It was beautifully sweet and perfectly balanced between octaves. I thought, "This is special."

Looking around, I saw Mary Bergin, talking to someone near the back of the hall. It was between sets of music, and a good time to approach her, so I went over and got her attention. She smiled when she saw me and said hello. I held out the whistle and said, "I wanted you to see this." Her eyes twinkled as she looked at it. That was the kind of whistle she played for many years before they stopped being produced.

"Try it," I said.

"Is it safe to play?" She asked.

"Yeah. I've worked on it."

We stepped outside and she started to play, at first a little hesitantly. Her eyes lit up and she played on awhile. As she handed it back, she said, "Wonderful." "Isn't it sweet?" I asked. "Lovely," she said. "Good on ye."

A little later, back at my table, Laura Byrne appeared. We chatted a minute and I handed her the whistle. "I want you to try this," I said. She played the whistle a long time, and beautifully. There, I could hear better than when Mary played it and I realized that was the best classic D Generation I had ever heard. Gorgeous.

After Laura had left and my table was quiet awhile, I began to think of angels. I've mentioned before, I don't see angels, but at times, I'm keenly aware of their benevolent presence.

"You brought me here to see that whistle, didn't you?" I asked. "Yes," I heard them say. (I can't explain how this works, but it's clear enough to me where the words are coming from.)

The rest of the day went true to form for these events. I did enough business, saw some old friends and heard more great music. I noticed, I didn't feel the slightest bit tired. The event was scheduled to run until six o'clock, though typically, the musicians onstage ignore the schedule and play on for another hour or two.

A little after five o'clock, I was getting a few more whistles ready, to keep the full selection of finished whistles out on the table. As I was chamfering the sharp edges off the toneholes on a brass tenor G tonebody, my X-acto knife slipped and pierced my left wrist exactly at the pulse point. Blood flooded out faster that I remember ever seeing from such a small cut. I covered it in less than a second with a tissue and held strong pressure against it with my right thumb.

I stood up and walked over toward a beverage vendor's stall. I told the first person I encountered, "I've cut myself and need a napkin. Can you help me?" The man pulled a clean cotton handkerchief from his pocket and handed it to me. "Perfect," I said. "I may have pierced my radial artery," I said. "I need to find a doctor or nurse."

He said, "I think Réidín Ó Flynn is around somewhere. Shall I look for her?" "I need someone to make an announcement from the stage," I said. "I don't think

Réidín's the best one for that." I walked toward the front of the hall thinking, "I need Paul Keating."

I found Paul and told him the situation. He went to the mic and made the announcement. Within a few minutes two women came to me where I had sat down. The whole time, I continued to hold strong pressure against the injury, using the handkerchief. There was no loss of blood.

I explained, "I may have pierced my radial artery." One of the women took the lead and did most of the talking. "If you have in fact done that, you need an ambulance." We discussed it for half a minute, and she took her cellphone and called 911. She seemed to know exactly what to do. I asked, "Are you a doctor?" "Nurse Practitioner," she said, as was the other woman there. (Later, I learned there were three nurse practitioners there, but I was only aware of two at the time.)

She got me to lie down on a platform near where I'd been sitting, found some duct tape to better attach the handkerchief, and helped me find a position where I could hold the wrist elevated and maintain pressure against the wound. After awhile, as we waited for the ambulance, she asked, "Why don't you take the pressure off and we'll see if the bleeding's stopped."

"I don't want to do that," I said. I had not released the pressure for as long as a second the entire time since the accident, and I was afraid to risk it.

Soon, two men in blue uniforms appeared.

We talked briefly, and they asked me to walk to the ambulance. "We need to know if you're dizzy or disoriented, see if you can walk a straight line, check your blood pressure." "I assume you mean not counting my baseline dizziness that I already had before this." "Right," they said.

We were walking as they told me this, so I said, "How about this straight line?" I walked along the line between two sections of pavement and surprised myself how easily I could do it, even with hands locked together so I couldn't hold my arms out. "Excellent," one of them said. Just at that moment, something came to me, clear as a light turning on. "I'm in better shape than I thought." From that moment, even in the midst of the emergency, I began to see the future differently.

When I got into the ambulance, I said, "This is nicer than my room."

"We want to start an IV," they said.

"If I may, I'll refuse that for now," I said. "I haven't lost any blood, and I'm sensitive to the phthalates in the tubing and IV bags. If it's necessary later we can do it, but I always feel worse after an IV." "It's up to you," they said.

Blood pressure was fine. Blood oxygen saturation in the fingers of both hands was 97% - 99% (better in the injured hand, actually) so there was no loss of circulation. No nerve damage. No tendon damage.

“Was there pulsing or a steady flow?” “A steady flow,” I said. “What color was the blood? Bright red or dark?” “Dark red.” “Then it wasn’t arterial blood. That would have been from a vein. There are many veins near the surface in that area that might have been involved.”

By then, we’d spent some time, and one of the men asked, “Let’s release the pressure and see if the bleeding’s stopped. Don’t move the bandage. If there’s a clot, you don’t want to disturb it. If it’s still bleeding it will soak the dressing and we’ll see it.”

There was no more blood. I didn’t want to take an ambulance ride in any case, but having seen the bleeding had stopped and appeared not to be from an artery, I decided I would have someone drive me to the emergency room in a car.

I felt well enough to go back to my table and spend some time working out logistics. Tom Wadsworth had already begun sorting out a ride to the nearest emergency room and looking for a place nearby I could stay the night. This was taking some time, and I began to feel it would be safe to remove the handkerchief and look at the cut. That would be important because I not only didn’t want to take an ambulance ride, I didn’t want to go to an emergency room.

I tracked down my nurse practitioner and asked her to sit with me as I removed the bandage. “I want you to be here while I do this,” I said. The cut was surgically clean, about half-an-inch-long and nicely closed, though fragile so soon after the injury. The incision was halfway across a medium sized vein just under the skin. I’d severed, or partially severed, that vein.

“OK,” I thought. “An urgent care center can handle this.” I told Tom and he started calling around to urgent care centers in the area. As he did that, I pondered, “At an urgent care center, what would they do? Butterfly bandage? Stitches?” And then it occurred to me. They would Superglue it. Arleen, my Better Half, had worked at an urgent care center. She’d Superglued many lacerations and cuts, including a few of mine here at the house. So I knew how it would be done. Not rocket science.

“They’re all closed,” Tom said. “Every one I try to call, the connection goes right to the ER.” “OK,” I said. “I think I’ve got this. I have some good Superglue here. I’ll do it myself. I think I can drive back to Connecticut OK.”

I glued the incision, exactly as Arleen had done for me now and then. I’m good with glue, use it all the time in my work, and I did a good job.

I didn't try to work on any more whistles and I got help packing and loading my car, but I was able to sit and enjoy the last hour of the concert, which ended at eight o'clock. I even sold another two or three whistles.

It was a perfect night for a drive. The air was pleasantly cool, with still some daylight for the first part of the two and a half hour trip. Traffic was light on the Interstates on a Saturday evening. I would be home exactly on schedule.

Just out of town, I saw a billboard, "Catskills Urgent Care Center, 9 am to 9 pm 365 days." I looked at the dashboard clock. Eight twenty eight pm. The nearest urgent care center was open, but somehow Tom hadn't been able to get through on the phone. "Thank you, Lord," I whispered. I didn't want to go on an ambulance OR to an emergency room OR to an urgent care center. I wanted to go home and sleep in my own bed.

As I drove, I thought about what had happened.

Arleen has always been impressed, almost to the point of awe, by how fast I knit and heal from injury. Patients she's seen would be incapacitated for days or weeks with injuries I recover from overnight or even sometimes, in hours.

Even with that background of experience I was impressed by how fast and well the cut had closed itself and knit together. And again I realized, "I'm in better shape than I thought."

"Angels," I thought. "You put me through this to show me, didn't you?"

"Yes, we did," The answer came back.

"Are you going to do this every time I start to doubt myself?" I asked.

"If we have to," the answer came.

Epilogue ...

I wondered if I'd overreacted, made a fuss about something trivial and put people to a lot of trouble unnecessarily. Just before I went to bed, I thought, "Where's the pulse?" I placed my index finger a millimeter below the incision, at the middle of the cut. Strong pulse. I placed my index finger a millimeter above the incision, at the middle of the cut. Strong pulse, and very close to the surface in both cases.

The incision was exactly over the radial artery, as I'd thought when I first cut myself. Truth be told, I believe I did pierce the radial artery with the point of that knife. I saw dark blood because I also opened a vein closer to the surface, and I didn't see pulsing because there was an additional steady flow from the vein and I covered the cut before the next heartbeat. I think the surgical cleanness of the cut and my strong capacity to heal are what allowed it to close as it did.

"It was necessary that there should be sin; but all shall be well, and all shall be well, and all manner of thing shall be well."

~ Julian of Norwich

Jul 19, 2017 7:50pm

Running errands this afternoon, it occurred to me, this is Wednesday. Half price on clothing day at the Salvation Army store.

As I stopped to turn into the parking lot, I saw a wiry man, tousled black hair and olive skin, pushing a bicycle. Hanging from the bicycle were two trash bags that appeared to be full of recyclable bottles and jugs.

I usually don't offer money to a homeless person unless they ask for it. But it was clear, this man needs money and was working hard for almost no money at all.

I called out, "Can you use some money?"

He called back, "No English," and turned away.

I pulled into the parking lot and called to him. "Come back," I said. "I have something for you." His back was turned and he was moving away. I was afraid he would flee, but he turned and came back toward my car.

In my pocket were a few bills still left from business at my vendor's table during Catskills Irish Arts Week. I looked for a twenty and handed it to him.

He looked like he might cry. "Thank you, thank you. Thank you, Sir," he said.

Jul 21, 2017 1:32pm

"Max," I said, "when you lick your chops, that means 'Can I have it?' right?"

"Correct," he said. "Now are you going to give me that thing or not?"

Jul 21, 2017 5:26pm

I lost count at eight barn swallows swooping and swirling over the driveway outside my office window. I know these birds. I watched two (or maybe there were three) of them grow up and disappear from their nest under the eaves at the front of the house.

Three more I watched, earlier in the season, as they lined up along the rain gutter above the deck, waiting for mom and dad to scoop up bugs over the hayfield and bring them back. The year before, there were five barn swallow kids lining up for supper.

Not many mosquitoes here. I thank the birds for that.

Jul 23, 2017 1:05pm

"It was a nice quiet afternoon session. She came in with her dad and her concertina. Shy. Sat on the outside. Asked her to play a tune after a while but she froze, went back to her dad. Tears. Went over later to chat and tell her not to worry. Asked her to come down the back of Cruises to play a tune with me on my own. Slowly, eventually we moved down. Sat alone with the instruments out but she still couldn't do it. Asked her to play 'The Boys of Bluehill' or something easy but nothing. Shy and humble. I was just about to leave it and then she started. Slowly. The finest G minor tune, played with rhythm and soul. Amazing music from this young girl. I don't know how she felt as we finished but I was seriously moved. And that's why I love music."

~ *Eoin O'Neill*

Jul 25, 2017 10:37pm

Time for Max to go out before bedtime. I find him with Natasha on her bed, intensely focused, watching her eat a sandwich. Amazing power of concentration, that dog has. No chance I'll be able to get him downstairs before Natasha finishes the sandwich.

"I'll go downstairs," she says.

"Great. He'll follow your sandwich."

And sure enough, he does, and he heads for the front door to go out. Then he notices, Natasha and her sandwich have gone back upstairs. He starts toward the stairs again. "No, Max! Come here," I call to him.

He comes back to the front door and we go out. He goes down the three front steps to the grass but keeps looking back at the door. He starts to go back up the steps. I call him and start to run out into the yard, hoping he'll follow. Max catches the spirit of the moment and runs to catch up with me.

"Whew," I think to myself. "That was complicated." Max, the sandwich forgotten, does his business. We go back inside and he bounds into the kitchen to claim his customary after-going-out treat.

Jul 28, 2017 4:01pm

The best way, I've learned, to find something you've lost, is to lose something else.

I went looking for my pruning saw and didn't find it, but I did find my crowbar which has been missing since last year.

Jul 31, 2017 10:42pm

"Every heart, every heart
to love will come
but like a refugee
Ring the bells that still can ring
Forget your perfect offering
There is a crack, a crack in everything
That's how the light gets in."

~ *Leonard Cohen, "Anthem"*

Aug 1, 2017 6:48am

6:10 am. I hear hinges creak as Max pushes my door open. His claws tap-tap-tap the oak floor as he approaches. Does he have his tug-of-war/throw-the-bear plush bear? I hope not. I'm not ready to open my eyes.

I feel Max's nose touch mine, sniffing breath, checking vital signs. I'm OK, Max. He jumps up on the bed and curls up next to me.

The Prequel

Life Before Max

Reminiscences from the New York homestead

Long ago in a farmhouse far away ...

There was a crunching sound in the pantry.

After a day or two of this, Arleen beckoned me into the pantry and said, "Do you hear that?"

I knew I was in trouble.

I flew into action. Jumped in the car and rushed out to get mouse-proof food containers. Got back home and packed all the pantry contents neatly in the mouse-proof containers. Proudly showed Arleen I'd solved the problem. I was a hero. I had saved the pantry from the mouse.

Well ...

Mouse gotta eat, mouse-proof containers or no mouse-proof containers.

The next morning, Arleen showed me where, during the night, the mouse had chewed a hole in her purse and eaten her chocolate.

Now I was in SERIOUS trouble.

The only solution, I determined, would be to train the mouse.

My workroom was on the same floor as the pantry, so I figured if I fed the mouse in my workroom, he'd stay out of the pantry and out of Arleen's purse. I set a tray on the floor a few feet away from my chair. On the tray, I put an empty, but not washed, peanut butter jar. Soon, the mouse discovered the jar and set about cleaning up the remaining bits of peanut butter. This was a big job for a mouse, and it took several days.

The children named him Ralph.

He was a vole, or meadow mouse. Ralph would keep me company every night, working on his peanut butter jar. The children ate a lot of peanut butter, so there was always a jar for Ralph to work on. From time to time, he would emerge from the jar, stand on his hind legs and make eye contact. Ralph was good company.

One day, after several weeks of this, I heard a familiar crunching sound in the pantry.

"Ralph! We talked about this. I thought we had an understanding!"

The crunching seemed to be coming from some flattened boxes that were going to be recycled. I picked up the top box, expecting to see a mouse scurry away. No mouse. The crunching continued, only interrupted for a few seconds by my rustling the boxes.

I picked up all the boxes. The crunching stopped, but no mouse scurried off.

All that was left was an empty Cheerios box that had been at the bottom of the pile. I thought, "He couldn't be in there."

I picked up the Cheerios box and looked inside. There was a wax paper bag inside that had held the cereal. I thought, "He couldn't be in that bag."

I pulled the bag out of the box, and there, standing on his hind legs with his forepaws against the side of the bag, was Ralph, gazing calmly at me from inside the bag.

I drove Ralph to the park and let him go in the woods.

I left the tray in place to lure any new mice away from the pantry and Arleen's chocolates.

Only a few days passed and another mouse showed up, this time a deer mouse.

That was Ralph II, the greatest mouse I ever knew. Ralph II kept me company as I worked into the night for several months until I began to see signs of another mouse and had to catch both of them. I was heartbroken when I let Ralph II go in the woods. (It's Ralph II whose picture is on every Freeman-tweaked whistle.)

After Ralph II, there was Gus, another vole. Gus was only with us for a week or two, but he was the hardest-working mouse of all. He would show up, not just at night, but in the middle of the day, working two shifts at the Global Pennywhistle Tweaking Research and Production Consortium Headquarters. Gus was so tame, the children could creep close to him and he wouldn't scurry. He'd stand on his hind legs and make eye contact, to their delight.

Then there was Mouse, the last rodent on the GPTR&PC Headquarters staff.

By the time Mouse came around, the arrangement had lost its novelty and I didn't pay much attention to him. He was a very shy animal, and I rarely saw him. An online friend had sent a supply of sunflower seeds for Mouse, which I left for him on the tray.

But Mouse wouldn't stay and eat. All night long, he would haul sunflower seeds from the tray to his secret cache somewhere. Back and forth, back and forth, over and over again, while I worked on whistles.

My online friends and I wrote a song for Mouse:

Gotta haul dem seeds,
Gotta haul dem seeds.
I'm a working MOUSE,
Gotta haul dem seeds.

One day, in the spring, I was looking for something in my workroom closet. I noticed a pair of shoes I hadn't worn much and wouldn't likely wear again. I thought, "I'll give these to the thrift store." I picked up one of the shoes, and out popped Mouse! As he scurried away, I looked inside the shoe.

There, inside the shoe was a cozy (and warm) little mouse nest, made of dryer lint and ...

my whiskers!

All winter long, as he was hauling seeds back and forth, whenever Mouse encountered a whisker that had fallen from my beard, he picked it up and tucked it into his shoe nest.

I've wondered about this. Why would a mouse make his nest in a shoe and insulate it with human whiskers? Well, to cover his own scent. "No mouse in here! I'm a big scary human, so you'd better beware!"

<u>*Circa 1880, afternoon*</u>

Mr. and Mrs. A.E. Olmstead, shortly after the house was built

We purchased the house from Chuck and Cathy Miller, who bought it from Mildred Drake, A.E. Olmstead's granddaughter. Mildred was in her nineties when we occupied the house her grandfather built. A few years before we moved in, that 100-plus-year-old maple tree fell and demolished the wrap-around porch. In the reconstruction, Chuck and Cathy installed a fireplace in the living room and put on a smaller porch. A stump four feet across remains where the tree stood.

Mildred's son, Phil Drake, lived on a farm down the road from us. In his seventies, Phil sold the farm to Ruben and Catherine Hershberger, who along with their children, brought it back to life as a working, family farm.

Phil ran a band saw sawmill in the barn on the property. When Ruben took over, he set up his own, ancient sawmill, which ran off a diesel engine. When I asked Ruben why he couldn't have just kept using Phil's band saw, he said, "Too many electronics."

When Ruben renovated the farmhouse, he removed all the wiring and most of the plumbing. In the kitchen, he installed a tank, filled by a gasoline powered pump that drew water from the well. From that tank, the family took all the water for the household. Eventually, Ruben pulled down the old barn and, in a traditional Amish barn raising, erected a magnificent new structure.

Sep 24, 2004 11:36am

In which Arleen accidentally becomes two dollars richer ...

OK, so Arleen and I are sitting at the kitchen table when we notice that Chucky from across the street is mowing our lawn.

It's a big lawn, a vacant lot, actually, that adjoins our house lot. Chucky and Aaron live with their parents across the street from it.

Chucky and Aaron are in their fifties, I would guess, never married, and something of a legend around here. They're two of the most cheerful people I've ever encountered. I suspect they're here on loan from another dimension, the abode of clowns, leprechauns and angels. That's the only way I can explain them.

As we watch Chucky mowing our lawn, I speculate that he might be trying out a lawn tractor he's been working on. Chucky and Aaron's front yard is full of old cars, lawnmowers and such, that they've dragged in from somewhere, put aright and then displayed for sale. This is something of a tradition around here. Chucky and Aaron do cars, lawn tractors, etc.; Dane, a couple of doors down, does snowmobiles, motorbikes, lawn tractors, etc.; and I, as you know, do house trailers.

On the other hand, the lawn needed mowing, and some of the neighbors have mowed that field occasionally to help us out. I figure maybe I should offer Chucky a few dollars for gas if it turns out he's doing it as a favor.

This must be done with a certain amount of care. If I give him enough money to make it worth his while, I may find him mowing the lawn when we don't want it mowed, expecting payment.

Arleen and I agree that three dollars is the correct amount. I determine that I have a five and a ten, but no ones. Arleen looks in her purse and finds three ones, which I take, giving her the five in exchange.

As we're conducting this transaction, I notice a plume of smoke coming from the lawn tractor. Equipped with the three dollars, I walk out to greet Chucky.

Looking toward where he had been mowing, I see the lawn is only half-mowed, but he and the lawn tractor have disappeared. Then, in their usual manner, Chucky and Aaron rematerialize on the spot by the time I get there. They don't come and go like normal humans. They materialize and dematerialize out of nowhere.

Chucky and Aaron couldn't be happier to see me. "Hi, Jerry!" "Hi, Jerry!" "Hi, Chucky. Hi, Aaron. Whatcha doin'?"

"Aw, I just rebuilt the engine on that tractor there and wanted to give it a try." (I congratulate myself for having guessed correctly.) "I coulda' mowed Van Ry's yard there but it's pretty small, so I figured I'd do this one."

"I saw some smoke. What happened?"

"Burned a belt."

"So I guess it won't work without a belt, then?"

"Three belts," Aaron says, grinning.

Chucky and Aaron seem perfectly delighted with the afternoon's events. This, in fact, is the only mood I've ever seen them in, no matter what the situation.

Anyway, with the three dollars still in my pocket, I say goodbye to Chucky and Aaron and return to the house, smiling. It's impossible to leave Chucky and Aaron without a smile.

"Well, Hon. It looks like you made two dollars," I tell Arleen.

Sep 25, 2004 2:19pm

Chapter two ...

Just now, I walk out to do some work on the house trailers and see Aaron on a green lawn tractor, mowing the rest of the lot Chucky started day before yesterday on a red one.

I walk over, and he shuts off the motor.

"Hi, Aaron."

"Hi, Jerry!"

"That's a different tractor, isn't it? The other one was red."

"This one's mine. The red one's Chucky's. I put new rings in, but it still isn't right. It should have more power."

"Will you sell it when it's fixed?"

"No. It's for me."

"That red one Chucky had, that's not the same red one I saw him with last fall, right?"

"Right."

"How many lawn tractors do you have?"

"I've got two. Chucky's got seven. He likes lawn tractors. This one still isn't right, though. It should have more power."

I make farewell noises and start to leave, but Aaron isn't done with me.

"Did you see the muffler I made?"

"No. Where?"

"Right here. See?" He points to some welded pipes at the front of the tractor.

"Wow. You did that? It's not loud at all."

"Nope." Then Aaron proceeds to tell me exactly how he made the muffler.

"OK, then. I'll see you, Aaron. Take care."

Aaron tries to start the lawn tractor, but it refuses.

"Uh oh," Aaron says, grinning broadly. "It won't start."

I feel slightly guilty, since he stopped the engine because I walked up to him, but I figure there's nothing I can do, and I don't want to spend the entire afternoon chatting with Aaron. So I continue my retreat.

"Maybe vapor lock," I hear him say enthusiastically.

I go about my business at the trailers. When I return, I see the mowing is complete. Aaron and the lawn tractor have vanished.

Aug 17, 2005 2:11pm

I found a horse ...

Yesterday, I had to do something to one of my house trailers, so I walked back to where I keep them.

As I arrived, I couldn't help but notice there was a pretty Belgian mare, a very large horse, standing in front of the trailer I wanted to work on, placidly nibbling the grass.

I thought to myself, "I don't remember that being there."

She was so nonchalant in the way she went about dining on the greenery, I actually wondered whether she was supposed to be there or not.

She allowed me to approach and take hold of her halter, so I led her toward my neighbor's pasture where she belongs. As I topped the rise and came in view of the pasture, I observed that the electric fence appeared intact. Not knowing anything about electric fences, I decided to take another route.

So I led this enormous horse down the main street of Orwell, New York, past several houses. At one house, a group of people was sitting on the front step, so I called to them, "Which house is the Carters'?"

"It's the house after next," I was told.

"They seem to have lost their horse," I said.

Jun 15, 2006 1:02pm

The children are bored

Jun 24, 2006 7:59pm

Here's something you can try ...

Visiting this evening with my neighbors the Hershbergers, conversation went to the topic of the wringer washing machine that had appeared in their yard.

I learned this one had been on loan to their recently married daughter, who now has her own washing machine. I have the electric motor that came off it. The Amish remove the electric motors and run their appliances with lawn mower engines.

Ananiah, at around 20 the oldest son still living at home, and one of the sweetest personalities I've ever encountered, told me a washing machine works very well for cleaning fish. Fill it with bluegills, run it awhile, and the scales come right off. I didn't ask, but I believe you are supposed to remove the clothes from the washing machine first.

Mar 14, 2007 11:38pm

Lucky had a big day yesterday

We had some digging done in the backyard. The excavating contractor, a neighbor with whom I've worked a lot, had brought his nine or so year old grandson with him, as well as two shovel guys.

I thought Lucky might amuse them, especially the boy, so I put him in my shirt pocket and walked out to where the crew and junior apprentice were putting together a list of things for me to pick up at the hardware store.

I walked up, writing pad in hand, Lucky in pocket, and announced, "I brought my assistant."

In unison, all four looked at me with puzzled faces, not seeing anyone else. Then, one by one, their faces lit up as they noticed Lucky peering out in "Kilroy was here" fashion over the top of my pocket.

"Wow, cool! A RAT!!" the boy exclaimed. "Can I hold him?"

So for the next few minutes, we discussed the rat. The excavating contractor petted Lucky's head inside my shirt pocket. I hauled Lucky out (always a battle;

Lucky loves my pocket) to predictable amazement at how big he is. He climbed up the boy's arm and perched on his shoulder.

I then put Lucky away and drove off with my utility trailer to get the needed items. I unloaded the items where the crew was working and went inside to get Lucky for the boy to play with again. When I arrived back at the site, the excavator told me the hardware store had given me the wrong pipe fitting, and could I go back and exchange it. He gave me a piece of the type of pipe the fitting needed to match, along with the mismatched fitting to exchange.

That presented a dilemma.

I didn't want to hold up the work, but Lucky was still in my pocket. After weighing the hassle of going back inside, getting past the dog (who barks and licks his chops when he sees him), and putting Lucky back in his cage, I decided to just jump in the car, Lucky in pocket, and go to the hardware store.

The ride to the store was uneventful. Lucky rode happily in my pocket, nose in the air, looking and sniffing with great interest.

When I got to the hardware store parking lot I observed a fragile-looking, elderly couple walking toward the door, and I realized I couldn't just walk in the store with a rat sticking out of my pocket. I saw a mental image of myself trying to explain why these two had fainted and needed to be resuscitated there on the blacktop.

I determined that I could carry the piece of pipe under my left arm, left hand curled over the pocket to hide Lucky, with the fitting in my right hand. This would look normal enough not to draw attention.

I walked into the store and went looking for Tina, the petite, long haired blond manager of the store, who knows more about roof repair, septic systems, drywall finishing, etc., than the next ten hardware store people combined.

I found her in the paint section, conferring with another employee.

I approached them, moved my hand away from Lucky's pocket and said, "Hi, Tina. I'd like you to meet my assistant."

They both looked at me with the standard puzzlement. Then Tina's eyes lit up with a conspirational twinkle, indicating she had spotted my rat. The two made a fuss over Lucky, and Tina and I discussed how I could conclude my transaction without setting any customers or employees screaming.

"I'll check you out," she said, and proceeded to a vacant cash register.

In that store, the checkout lines are in pairs, with the cashiers side by side about three feet apart, facing counters in opposite directions.

The adjacent register was being tended by another female employee with whom I've done a lot of business. There were no customers at her counter. Tina tugged the cashier's sleeve and whispered, "Jerry, show Jamie."

I moved my hand away from Lucky's pocket, and Jamie lit up with delight. She and Tina fussed over Lucky for awhile more, both of them alight with the same conspirational twinkle. Then I concluded my transaction and exited the store.

On the way home, Lucky decided he was bored. For a short time, a running battle ensued as he tried to climb out of my pocket and I kept trying to push him back in.

Then I figured out I only needed to hold my hand over the top of my pocket. The warmth of my hand, my scent masking any interesting ambient scents, and the darkness being far preferable to daylight for a rat, all combined to get him to settle down and stay put.

I went into the house and handed Lucky off to Genia, fourteen, who was sitting at the computer in the living room. Then I went back to the worksite to deliver the correct fitting.

May 21, 2007 7:52pm

Can't get no respect ...

OK, so the five-year-old's first baby tooth comes out, amid much excitement among her siblings.

Arleen's off visiting her mother, during which time I've been going through the house and freshening up a few things she'll be pleased to discover when she gets back.

So after the small children have gone to bed, and with the big ones detailed to babysit in my absence, I head out to get some things for the house. I come back with a new oriental-style rug for the dining room, a soft checkerboard-pattern rug for the room the little ones share, a set of three new nonstick skillets, a new 13-inch television for the kitchen and a desk lamp for the ten-year-old. I arrange the skillets on the stovetop and distribute the other treasures to their various destinations.

Next morning the children clamor into my bedroom, all excited.

Wow! You should see all the cool stuff the TOOTH FAIRY left us!!!

Jun 16, 2007 9:30pm

Arleen and the children were away, and I was alone in the house.

The sky was clear and sunny, and the power went out. I thought, "That doesn't make sense. It's a nice day." I had the radio on, and there had been no weather advisories.

Within just a few minutes, the sky was dark. It got dark faster than I've ever seen before. It started to rain and thunder, then very suddenly I heard a wind like I've never heard before. A steady, very loud hiss/whistle, very strong, very steady like a tremendous river of wind. I thought, "Is this a tornado? No sound like a freight train, must be something else."

Then a large maple tree, probably 100 years old, in the front yard blew down, and I ran to the basement. From there, I could watch out a small window at the top of the foundation wall but I couldn't see much.

I was afraid my mobile homes had been destroyed (I have two of them here, both sold but not delivered yet), so as soon as I saw it wasn't blowing so strongly any more, I went out into the storm to check.

No, the mobile homes were OK. As it turns out, the wind hit them end on, which they could take. If they had been hit broadside, they would have been blown off their blocks and ruined.

Later, I was at the post office, which is a tiny box of a wood building about 100 yards from here. It was a public tea house in the 1800's. In its present incarnation, it's perfectly suited as the post office for a village of 350 souls.

Renee, the postmistress, had been there during whatever it was. She said she couldn't figure out where to go. The wind was rattling the front door, so she stood there trying to hold it shut. She could see out the door's window, and saw that all the trees, even huge old trees, were bowed over sideways, horizontal to the ground, the wind was so strong.

Reuben Hershberger and his sons were out in it. They ran for shelter and huddled against the leeward side of a little wooden shed, which had been the closest thing they could reach. They watched it blow down a block wall where they were renovating the old barn, and they watched it blow away a silo top they had on the ground by the barn.

Very strange weather. Not a tornado, but not typical thunderstorm gusts, either. Extremely strong wind (I would say 80 - 100 miles per hour) blowing steadily in a straight line, not swirling, for some length of time. I can't say how long. It could have been only half a minute, or it could have been several minutes. I just don't know.

I have the sense that Chucky and Aaron are forces of nature themselves. The image that arose seeing them materialized there before the fallen tree was of termites. Tropical termites, maybe, that somehow sense a tree somewhere in the jungle has fallen and swarm to it within minutes, maybe even seconds, of the catastrophe.

I knew why they were there.

We had the relevant conversation, and it was agreed that Chucky and Aaron would come the next day and saw up the fallen tree. Firewood. Later in the day, another neighbor came around and asked if he could take the tree for firewood, but I had to tell him Chucky and Aaron had asked for it first.

Sep 05, 2007 6:36pm

I just came back from sitting on the front step with Mattie and Ezra Schwartzentruper, one of 17 Amish families who've moved here in the last two years. Their little niece Rebecca was with them. Shy, she kept a little back from the grownups as I sat with them. She was by turns gleeful and despondent as a cat submitted to being held for awhile and then escaped.

I discussed the naming of animals with Ezra. He reported that they name horses, cows, and sometimes dogs, but they haven't gotten around to naming their cow yet.

I pointed out that this isn't something you can be too busy to do. You couldn't say, "I didn't get a chance to name the cow because I had to bring in the hay." Ezra admitted that was so.

I told him I have two animals, both of which have names, Lucky and Jack. He didn't seem at all surprised or bewildered (unlike most Amish I've told this) when I explained that Lucky and Jack are rats.

Next time I visit them (which will be Monday to get more of their tomatoes and melons), I'll be interested to find out if they've corrected their oversight and named the cow. And I'll bring Lucky, who loves to go visiting. (No cat jokes, please. I'll deal with her, and Lucky will be fine.)

Sep 05, 2007 6:54pm

Someone commented: "The best thing to do is for YOU to give the animal a name. Naming rights I would call it."

Oh, this is a good idea!

Please, everyone, suggest names. Then, if they haven't named her by Monday evening, I can offer to name her for them. At no charge, of course.

This is a Jersey cow who's extremely friendly. I haven't been around cows a lot, but she seems like an especially sweet-natured animal. I would love to be the one who named her.

The Amish shy away from anything that might be interpreted as ostentatious or attention-getting. There's an almost Buddhist non-self centeredness about their approach that's refreshing to encounter.

The Amish animals whose names I've been told are two standard-bred buggy horses named Nancy and Alice, a Belgian draft horse named Henry, and a Percheron draft horse named Ben.

Sep 08, 2007 6:22pm

The Schwartzentruper's Jersey cow is now named Betsy.

I found Ezra, his brother Peter and another Amish man I didn't recognize sitting around the drop front secretary desk in the large room of the house. Ezra was smoking his pipe.

I asked Ezra if he thought it would be OK to name the cow Betsy.

He asked, "Why do you want to name her Betsy?"

I said, "I think Betsy would be a good name for her. Can we name her Betsy?"

He said, "I don't care what we call her. It doesn't matter what you call an animal."

I said, "It sounds like you don't lie awake at night worrying that you've given your animals the wrong names."

They laughed.

I said, "OK. I'll name her Betsy. And I won't charge you anything. In fact, I'll name any animal you need to have named, and I'll do it for free!"

They laughed. Peter said, "Maybe you could name my calf."

OK ...

What shall we name Peter's calf? I may see him again either tomorrow or Wednesday. If I do, I'll find out more about the calf; at least what breed she is.

Sep 09, 2007 3:19pm

Someone commented: "I'm impressed by the name 'Ezra Schwartzentruper.'"

They're newly married, so it's just Ezra and Mattie. Schwartzentruper's a common name among that branch of Amish. They're "Schwartzentruper Amish," which is the most conservative branch.

Closer down the road are the Hershbergers: Ruben, Caroline and their children, Jacob, Naomi, Jonah, Rachel, Noah, Ananiah, Ruben and Levi.

Sep 10, 2007 8:41pm

This evening, I visited with Ezra for a few minutes. I determined that the calf isn't Peter's, but Jacob's. In the dim light on the evening we named Betsy, I mistook who was speaking.

I suggested that Jacob name his calf Molly. Ezra indicated he thought Molly would be a good name for Jacob's calf and would pass the information along to Jacob. He seemed appreciative.

Jan25, 2008 9:26am

"You girls have watched enough videos today. Find something else to do."

May 8, 2008 6:14pm

Today I stood with my Amish neighbor Levi Zook on the porch overlooking his pasture. As we watched, his three goats marched toward a spot in an overgrown area at one side of the field. We couldn't see what the object of interest was, but the goats clearly knew where they were going and to what purpose.

"I've heard goats can be a lot of trouble," I said. "Is that true?"

"Well, you know what they say about goats," Levi replied slowly. "Everybody should have a goat one time, because that way they can always enjoy how nice it is NOT to have a goat."

Appendix

Tin Whistles

In case you're still interested to know more ...

Jerry Freeman tweaked whistles are available
through www.freemanwhistles.com

Here are two explanatory pieces I hand out at my vendor's table.

The first piece is a simple overview of the work I do and the different whistles I offer.

The second piece I wrote because some people want to know every intricate detail of what I do to each whistle. At music events I got hoarse explaining over and over again, so I wrote "How I Tweak a Whistle."

Jerry Freeman is the world's only full time, professional penny whistle tweaker.

"Tweaking" a penny whistle is much like setting up a guitar or fiddle; it is the process of making fine adjustments and modifications to get the best possible performance from the instrument.

Jerry takes mass-produced whistles and adjusts the soundblade position, windway exit geometry, voicing chamber and tonebody to create affordable instruments that many consider not simply outstanding whistles for the modest cost, but outstanding whistles at any cost.

Jerry offers tweaked Generations*, including his unique, key of A and low G tweaked Generations and his own creations, the widely acclaimed Blackbirds** and Mellow Dogs**.

Mellow Dogs are wide-body whistles available in D and as a D/C set (one whistlehead with two tubes). Blackbirds are standard-body whistles in Eb, D and C.

Blackbirds and Mellow Dogs are noted for their pure-drop, authentic, traditional voicings that favor a birdlike, sweet timbre in a very responsive, clean-playing instrument.

Blackbird: Sweetest/purest voicing, takes gentlest air on the bottom notes.

Tweaked Generation: Sweet voicing, but warmer, more complex, takes medium air, based on preferred, classic pre-1980's Generation voicing.

Mellow Dog: Bigger sound, great all-purpose whistle, including bigger sessions, takes more push at the top notes.

* Generation is a brand of whistle made in England since at least the early 20th century. The first Generation whistles were all-metal with a lead plug in the mouthpiece. Later the lead was replaced by another, presumably less toxic, metal.

Generation introduced injection-molded plastic whistleheads around 1953. Those Generations (~ 1953 to early 1980's) were the most popular whistles for Irish traditional music and formed the basis for what is considered the "pure-drop authentic" Irish whistle sound. In the early 1980's, Generation replaced their injection molding tooling, resulting in somewhat different voicings (more edgy, less pure and birdlike). Vintage, pre-1980's Generations are still in use and are highly prized.

** I make Blackbirds and Mellow Dogs from whistles manufactured by Feadog in Ireland. My Blackbirds and Mellow Dogs are nothing like the Feadogs I start with, so I've given them their own names. I don't call them "tweaked Feadogs" because people would expect them to be like Feadogs, which they are not.

How I tweak a whistle

Here are some of the issues with mass-produced whistles:

1. There are shapes that can't be made with an injection mold. Undercuts will lock the molded part inside the mold, making it impossible to open the mold without damaging the part. Because of that, the whistlehead designs have been compromised so whistleheads can be mass produced using injection molding machines.

2. The hollow underneath the windway does not serve a musical function. It is there because a plastic part must avoid large variations in wall thickness to prevent "sinking," which is the distortion caused when hot plastic cools and thicker areas shrink more than thinner ones.

3. The "step" is never correct in these whistles. If the bottom of the soundblade is above the windway floor, that is a positive step. If the bottom of the soundblade is exactly even with the windway floor, that is zero step, and if the bottom of the soundblade is below the windway floor, that is a negative step.

Here's what I do when I tweak a whistle:

~ I remove the whistlehead. With some keys of whistle, I enlarge the socket to fit the tube correctly so it can be more easily tuned.

~ I fill the cavity under the windway. What material you use matters. Many people use poster putty, which does clean up some of the buzzes and squawks but it also tends to deaden the sound. For tweaked Generations, I've developed a lattice construction that is transparent to sound waves, but acts like a solid wall to the flowing air. Blackbirds and Mellow Dogs are best with a hard, dense material to fill the cavity so for these I use an epoxy resin.

~ In mass-produced whistleheads, where the windway floor meets the voicing chamber, there is a square edge, which is incorrect. It is done because an appropriately chamfered or rounded edge would be an undercut and make the whistlehead impossible to remove from the mold. I correct that by working a radius onto the end of the windway floor.

~ I laminate a thickness of plastic underneath the soundblade to correct the step, the soundblade position relative to the windway floor. I place the lamination differently in different whistles to achieve the different voicings that distinguish Blackbirds from tweaked Generations, etc. I've modeled the tweaked Generation's voicing to match as closely as possible the classic voicing of the Generation whistles that were produced between the middle 1950's and the early 1980's when Generation replaced their tooling and the whistles changed.

~ I press a brass ring around the whistlehead socket to protect it from cracking from the pressure of the tube inside. That has always been the demise of these mass-produced whistles. Occasionally you see a performer playing an old whistle that has electrician's tape wrapped around a cracked socket.

~ Depending on the key and model of whistle, I remove material from one or both ends of the tonebody to bring the bell note into tune and increase the range the whistle can be tuned. Mellow Dog, alto A tweaked Generation and tenor G Generation tonebodies I make myself.

It bears mention, some of these adjustments are interrelated. If I change one of them another adjustment will need to be modified to make it work correctly. If you were to only do one or two of the tweaks, even if you could duplicate them exactly, you would not get the same result.

I hope that makes sense.